Ex-Library: Friends of
Lake County Public Library

P9-DMZ-650

TARGET T●KYO

Books by James M. Merrill

THE REBEL SHORE:
The Story of Union Sea Power in the Civil War

QUARTER-DECK AND FO'C'S'LE

UNCOMMON VALOR

TARGET T●KYO

The Halsey-Doolittle Raid

BY JAMES M. MERRILL

RAND McNALLY & COMPANY
Chicago   New York   San Francisco

LAKE COUNTY PUBLIC LIBRARY

12231932

Copyright © 1964 by James M. Merrill
Copyright 1964 under International Copyright Union
by James M. Merrill

First Printing August 1964
Library of Congress Catalog Card Number: 64-21328
Printed in the United States of America
by Rand McNally & Company

For Dr. and Mrs. William Alexander McIntosh

PREFACE

RESEARCHING MATERIALS FOR WORLD WAR II history is more complicated and more demanding than hunting down sources for earlier wars. The historian must play the multiple roles of sleuth, diplomat, interviewer, letter writer; pass a battery of loyalty tests and be fingerprinted in order to gain access to classified documents; learn to read microfilm rapidly and to operate a tape recorder efficiently. He discovers that most governmental agencies like the National Archives and the Navy Department are extremely co-operative, anxious to pull out and declassify materials which twenty years ago were marked "SECRET."

The records and information relating to the Halsey-Doolittle Raid are scattered throughout this country and Japan. When I first decided to write the story of this attack, I sent letters to former Whittier College students who reside in the Tokyo area. I contacted friends of friends in Japan; wrote the Japanese Consul General in Los Angeles; placed advertisements in the *New Japanese American News,* urging individuals who remembered the raid to get in touch with me.

Letters arrived. Two former students in Tokyo, Kazuko Suzuki and Kazuo Ohno, spent the summer of 1963 interviewing individuals by tape recorder. A Japanese student at Whittier College, Taki Kimoto, translated the tapes and letters. From this material plus the Tokyo newspapers for 1942 and the reports of the Japanese governmental censors, which are housed in the Orientalia Section, Library of Congress, I pieced together the Japanese side.

Official documents on the Navy's participation are in the Classified Operational Archives at the Washington Navy Yard under the auspices of the Director of Naval History. It is pleasant to work there. The Navy furnishes the researcher with typewriter, paper, pencils, and an assistant who cheerfully carts out the files and directs you to the coffee mess.

Manuscript materials on Air Force participation are located in the National Archives, Washington, D. C., and in the World War II Records Center, Alexandria, Virginia. The staffs were cordial and helpful in supplying me with research aids, pulling out long-buried boxes of records, and suggesting where additional information might be found. An important document is Doolittle's official report and the attached action reports of airmen. When the fliers arrived at Chungking, Intelligence Officer Colonel Merian Cooper debriefed them. This Cooper Report is almost the complete story of the raid. Beside the individual reports, Cooper analyzed the training, voyage, bomb run, and the escape. Important to the writing of this book is the secret history of the raid by S. L. A. Marshall. This document was lent to the Records Center, Alexandria, by the Office of Military History, Department of the Army.

To reconstruct the actions of the captured airmen, I

studied the official transcripts of the testimony taken at the various war crimes trials held by the International Military Tribunal, Far East. These sources are under the aegis of the State Department, but located both at the National Archives and the Alexandria Records Center.

To interview personnel in the United States, I either traveled to them or questioned them over the telephone. With one or two major exceptions, I discovered that the personal interview was practically worthless. Almost 25 years after the event, people forget.

The complete bibliography of the records, magazine articles, and books which I consulted in the preparation of this work is given at the conclusion.

James M. Merrill
Whittier College.

ACKNOWLEDGMENTS

My personal thanks go to the Doolittle raiders who co-operated with me on this book, especially to my friend Lieutenant Colonel H. F. Watson, USAF (ret.), who acted as technical advisor. Special thanks also go to John Taylor of the Army-Air Force Branch, National Archives, who was the first to uncover the official documents which made this book possible. I am also appreciative of the efforts of the following individuals who, in one way or another, assisted me in the research and preparation of the manuscript: Kazuko Suzuki and Kazuo Ohno of Obirin Junior College, Tokyo, who interviewed countless numbers of Japanese civilians; Florence Wells, Tokyo; Elbert L. Huber, Victor Gondos, and W. J. Nigh of the National Archives; Admiral E. M. Eller, Director of Naval History, and Dean Allard of his staff; Alan Thompson and Hisao Matsumoto, Library of Congress; Royal D. Frey and his staff, Air Force Museum, Wright-Patterson Air Force Base; Albert F. Simpson, Aerospace Studies Institute, Maxwell Air Force Base; Albert W. Upton, Benjamin Whitten, Ellsworth Lewman, and Taki Kimoto, all of Whittier College. My wife, Ann, helped immeasurably to complete this book.

CONTENTS

Illustrations between pages 112 and 113

TARGET T●KYO

REHEARSAL

THREE AND A HALF MONTHS AFTER THE HOLO-
caust at Pearl Harbor, late March 1942, seamen on the
deck of the United States submarine *Thresher* hooked
up fueling hoses in the heat and glare of Midway Island.
The sounds of surf and screeching seagulls muted the
clang of the black gang below as they repaired leaks
and tinkered with the engines prior to the *Thresher's*
departure for war patrol into Japanese waters. At 1305
hours the *Thresher* cast off lines from the fueling dock,
maneuvered down the channel out into the Pacific and
changed course to 270°. Below in his compartment, Lieutenant Commander William L. Anderson, USN, tore
open his secret orders and read—hunt down and sink
enemy shipping. On 14 April begin search for Japanese
surface craft which might intercept Task Force 16. A day
later the submarine *Trout* headed out of Midway on a
similar mission.

Out in the Pacific the freighter *Thomas Jefferson*, Navy-
manned, thrashed through heavy seas, steaming toward be-

leaguered Corregidor in the Philippines, the last United States bastion in the Far East. Since the first of the year Japanese planes had dumped bomb load after bomb load on The Rock and its begrimed American defenders. Colonel Paul Bunker, commanding the 59th Coast Artillery, felt the earth heave, stared at the denuded barracks, marked the gaping craters and the burned-out mechanic shops.

General Douglas MacArthur, commanding the American forces, issued bulletin after bulletin—"No further retreat! Thousands of men and hundreds of planes are enroute to help us!" In that inferno, Paul Bunker looked at the blazing sky and questioned. Why didn't the Americans and British mount a counter-offensive against enemy-held islands? Where were all the allied planes? Why hadn't Japan proper been bombed?

An American B-25, medium bomber, hurtled across the Texas countryside, ducking beneath telephone wires, the belly of the plane inches off the ground. Flocks of sheep, herds of cattle, and barnyard chickens all panicked at the B-25's approach. As the airmen ripped across woodlands, tree tops whipped past their ears and, peering out the windows, they saw the intricate patterns of bare branches. Lieutenant Don Smith saw a tractor in the yard, a truck in the road, a clutch of roofs.

Startled from a deep sleep by the ear-splitting howl, rancher James Martin rushed out of his farmhouse, and gazed up. Noticing his cattle running helter-skelter, he suddenly shook his fist at the fast-disappearing plane. In Texas, in New Mexico, in Kansas, other farmers toppled from bed to witness the ground-skipping bombers blurring across their lands, hell-bent for destiny.

These Mitchell bombers were the first units of Special

Bombing Project No. 1 which, on 18 April 1942, were to rain devastation on Tokyo.

[Since The Day of Infamy, 7 December 1941, President Franklin D. Roosevelt had been eager for the Army and Navy to strike at the very heart of Japan, deliver the destruction of war to the Japanese people, retaliate for Pearl Harbor. But along every shore bounding the China Sea, the defensive structure of the allies was crumbling. Americans watched the Japanese armies coil, strike, poise, coil again, and strike again as bases fell one by one.]

By the end of December 1941, the Japanese had, after clobbering the United States Navy at Pearl Harbor, knocked out for all practical purposes the Far Eastern Air Command, forced the American Asiatic Fleet from the Philippines into the Dutch East Indies, virtually sealed off General Douglas MacArthur's troops on Bataan and Corregidor, and were completing the encirclement of the Philippines. The enemy splashed ashore in Borneo, the initial step in their drive on the fabulously rich Dutch East Indies.

The British garrison at Hong Kong surrendered. Japanese penetrated Thailand, where, encountering meager resistance, they started mustering a force to thrust into Burma and the Malay States, a force that would ultimately march into Rangoon and Singapore.

Australia and New Zealand girded for invasion. In the United States public wrath over Pearl Harbor shifted to concern over American naval posture in the Pacific, a concern intensified by the death of the British battleships *Prince of Wales* and *Repulse* off Malaya in the Gulf of Siam. Americans imagined the enemy in Asia to be a subhuman species plodding unbelievable distances

19

on a spoonful of rice and a cup of tea. False air-raid alerts and rumors of enemy carriers lurking off the West Coast reflected America's unease.

On Saturday night, 10 January 1942, on board the flagship *Vixen,* anchored in the Potomac River, Admiral Ernest J. King, Chief of Naval Operations, and his staff sat in gloom, discussing how the Navy might deliver a savage and devastating blow at Japan. Carrier strikes against Marcus and Kwajalein Islands were all very well, but they scarcely had the fury or impact of Pearl Harbor. How could Japan be reached? Allied intelligence knew that enemy land-based planes were capable of patrolling 300 miles off shore; picket boats were already policing 500 miles out. How could carriers pierce this double cordon without meeting the fate of the *Prince of Wales?* Navy dive bombers lacked the range to attack from further away. Captain Francis Low, King's operations officer, then suggested a fantastic idea. Why not launch long-range Army bombers from the deck of a carrier?

In the Navy Department the next day, Sunday, the admiral's air officer, Captain Donald W. Duncan, sat locked in his office and masterminded a detailed plan in long hand. The mission was so secret, the element of surprise so essential, that he did not trust his yeoman to type the rough draft. A raid against Japan would revitalize Allied morale, reasoned the captain, confuse and impede Japanese war production, and reduce enemy pressure in other theaters when troops were withdrawn to defend the homeland.

To execute the mission, the planes' minimum requirements were a cruising radius of 2400 miles with a bomb load of 2000 lbs. Although both the B-26 and the B-23 satisfied the cruising range and bomb load requirements, the take-off characteristics of the B-26 were inadequate for carrier operations, and the large wing span of the B-23 meant that fewer planes could be accommodated on board a carrier. The assignment fell to the B-25, which had the punch and the range.

Duncan proposed that a high-speed task force run to within 500 miles of the Japanese coast, launch its bombers, and clear the area; the planes flying to selected military targets in the Tokyo-Yokohama, Osaka-Kobe, and Nagoya areas. To escape detection and antiaircraft fire, to assure accurate bombing of vital targets, he urged an extremely low-altitude strike. After delivering their eggs, the bombers were to head for airfields in eastern China, such as Chuchow, to land and refuel before pushing on to the strong Chinese base at Chungking in central China. The greatest nonstop distance any plane would have to fly would be 2000 miles. If the Soviet Union, then allied with the United States against Nazi Germany, but not against Japan, would accept 16 B-25s on Lend Lease at Vladivostok, the problems relating to the raid would be simplified.

After studying meteorological conditions, Duncan stressed that the sooner the planes pulled out for Japan the better. By the end of April, the prevailing weather conditions would become increasingly unfavorable.

Working and reworking the approach, the bomb run, the get-away, the captain went through the whole rigmarole again and again. The scheme looked good on paper, almost foolproof. He had calculated the risk commensurate with the results to be expected. It all stacked up as a valid, sane, although hazardous undertaking. Duncan believed in the mission. So did Admiral King.

The admiral was ushered into the office of General

H. H. "Hap" Arnold, Air Chief of Staff, at the Pentagon. Arnold listened as King elucidated Duncan's analyses and plans. The more the admiral bent his powers of persuasion, the more excited the general became. Arnold agreed enthusiastically to organize and equip the air units.

Twenty-four hours later, huge cranes at the operation dock in Norfolk Navy Yard placed two B-25s onto the flight deck of the carrier *Hornet*. She got under way, steaming eastward out to sea. Once in launching position, a bomber with a Navy pilot at its controls roared down the deck and took off into a stiff wind. "Well it's just another damn Navy experiment," snorted a veteran boatswain's mate, gaping at the sight. After this successful launch, the *Hornet* reversed course and headed back to Norfolk, where she immediately began taking on stores.

Hap Arnold picked Lieutenant Colonel James H. Doolittle to command the air units for the historic mission. Already a legend at 46, this short, lean Californian was regarded by many aviators as the best pilot in the air. Not only had Doolittle been a stunt man and racer in the hairy days of aviation, but he was a painstaking, brainy man, who had a sound knowledge of aerodynamics and held a science degree from Massachusetts Institute of Technology. The selection of Doolittle was a natural one. He had nerve, technical ability, and was a leader who could get the job done.

When Jimmy Doolittle walked into Arnold's office, the general without hesitation snapped, "Will you bomb Tokyo?"

"Yes, sir," Doolittle shot back.

"All right," said the general, "Go to it. I'll tell you the

guts of the plan. Then it's up to you to carry the ball. I'll back you up, win, lose, or draw."

After listening intently to Arnold, Doolittle disappeared to his hotel room in Washington. He reworked the proposed operation, concluded, as Duncan had done, that the B-25 could carry the bacon, and hastened back to the Pentagon. The Air Chief sat reading a report from Duncan on the B-25's successful launch from the *Hornet*. Captain Duncan was to work out the details of ship movement and task force organization. Doolittle was responsible for equipping and manning the aircraft. The general suggested that the 17th Bombardment Group and the 89th Reconnaissance Squadron, both undergoing B-25 combat training in South Carolina, should be the source of the mission's personnel.

At Wright Field in Ohio, Doolittle and Lieutenant Clare Bunch, aeronautical engineer, worked feverishly calculating ways to lighten the B-25 and to increase its gas capacity. By modifying, clearing out the non-essentials, the colonel took off fully loaded within a 500-foot space. He sped back to Washington.

When Doolittle arrived at the Pentagon, the entire nation was jarred by the news from the Far East. Singapore had fallen. In mid-February 1942, the enemy occupied virtually all the areas of importance in Borneo and the Celebes and was knocking out the chief Dutch stronghold on Amboina. Paratroopers swooped into Sumatra. Planes from Admiral Chuichi Nagumo's carriers raided Darwin, the principal port of northern Australia. Japanese naval units obliterated a force of American, British, Dutch, and Australian cruisers and destroyers in the Java Sea. The sons of Nippon landed on Java, the richest and most highly-developed island in the Dutch East Indies.

Allied forces elsewhere in the Pacific were bolstering the line they were determined to hold. Although the United States Navy was on the defensive, strategy was far from passive. Rear Admiral Frank Jack Fletcher's carrier force jabbed at Makin in the northern Gilberts and Jaluit and Mili in the southern Marshalls. Vice Admiral William F. Halsey's *Enterprise* group maneuvered farther into the Marshalls to hammer Wotje, Maloelap, and Kwajalein. With the situation in the southwest Pacific critical, Halsey hit Wake Island with planes from the *Enterprise* group and then, penetrating to within less than 1000 miles of Tokyo, attacked Marcus Island.

Three enlisted men wearing fatigues looked up from their work on the complex engine. The Carolina sun was low in the sky, and the faces of all three were coated with sweat and dirt. A gust of wind brought a shower of dust and small pebbles, and the men cursed as they wiped their eyes. Around them were the noise and activity of Lexington Field, Columbia, South Carolina. Along the parking apron more fatigue-clad GIs monkeyed with parked aircraft.

Looking high above the circling traffic pattern, they watched a lone plane make its approach. Nearby, Captain Ross Greening and Major Jack Hilger, both B-25 pilots attached to the 17th Bombardment Group, stood outside the mess hall and saw the bomber land and taxi to the control tower. Out climbed a short man with the oak leaves of a lieutenant colonel.

"For God's sake, it's Doolittle," Greening exclaimed.

"What in hell is The Little Man doing here?" Hilger drawled.

[The Little Man was seeking volunteers. The project, Doolittle explained, would be extremely hazardous, require a high degree of skill, and be of great value to the nation. "That's about all I can tell you about the mission now," finished Doolittle.

[Every pilot on the base responded. More enlisted men than the colonel needed stepped forward. These were ordinary airmen. The gunners, almost to a man, had never fired a machine gun from a plane. The navigators had the rudiments, but no practical experience. None who volunteered that day was schooled in combat or seasoned by action. None of the crews had worked together as a unit. They were not the cream of the Air Corps, not the chosen, but brave men who chose.]

But although they were inexperienced, these flying men were to pit their guts against the weather, mechanical failure and, perhaps, explosive death. They had survived rugged physical, psychological, and dexterity tests. They had overcome the challenge of increasingly complex aircraft. They had faced up to check rides, accelerated training programs, sudden emergencies. They had learned to live with fear of failure and had conquered it.

Two nights later in a hotel suite in Minneapolis, officers and men of a squadron from 17th Bombardment, then enroute to Lexington Field, listened to Captain David Jones. Davey had been at Wright Field with Edward J. "Ski" York, squadron commander. He said casually, "Captain York wanted me to talk to you and see how many of you would volunteer for a special mission. It's dangerous, important, and interesting."

"Well, what is it?" asked a lieutenant.

"I can't tell you," Jones replied. "I don't even know, myself."

Again, emphasizing he didn't have any poop as to destination, he said, "Who'll volunteer? It's perfectly all right if you don't. It's strictly up to you."

They all volunteered.

Within a week 24 crews, picked haphazardly by Doolittle, received orders to fly to Eglin Field, Valparaiso, Florida, for a final course of training.

When the aviators first climbed into the fuselage of the modified B-25, what they saw made them wince—the interior looked like a Rube Goldberg contrivance. Rummaging through the ships, the airmen noted the installation of three extra gasoline tanks: the first, a 225-gallon, leak-proof affair, fitted into the bomb bay, leaving room beneath for four 500-lb. bombs; the second, a rubber bag contraption of 160 gallons, lodged in the crawlway, blocking the one fore-and-aft passage through the ship, but with fittings to collapse the tank when empty; the third, holding 60 gallons, took up the space normally filled by the lower turret. This auxiliary supply and the 646 gallons in the main tanks plus 50 gallons to be carried along in tins gave each plane a 1141 gallon capacity.

The pilots gawked at the two wooden sticks simulating .50-caliber guns protruding from the extreme tip of the tail, a ruse to forestall enemy attack from that quarter. Steel blast plates were installed after the colonel discerned that the upper turret guns, when firing aft with muzzles close to the fuselage, popped rivets and tore the skin loose. With the lower turret removed, the bomber's armament was reduced to one .30-caliber machine gun in the nose, and two .50 calibers in the upper turret.

Up in the nose in the bombardier's compartment, the aviators found the Norden bombsight missing. In its place was the "Mark Twain," a simplified, 20-cent instrument designed by Captain Greening. It was a vertical plate with gradations marking elevations and a slide which moved up and down. Doolittle substituted this mechanism, since all bombing was to be done at extremely low altitudes.

Armorers equipped the planes with special 500-lb. demolition bombs, loaded with a mixture containing 50% TNT and 50% Amatol, armed with 1/10-of-a-second nose fuses and 1/40-of-a-second tail fuses, and special 500-lb. incendiary clusters containing 128 incendiary bombs.

Sun streamed through the windows of the operations shack at Eglin Field as 140 pilots, co-pilots, navigators, bombardiers, and gunners talked in small groups. The Little Man walked in. The crews lapsed into silence.

"If you men have any idea that this isn't the most dangerous thing you've ever been on," said Doolittle, "don't even start this training period. You can drop out now. There isn't much sense wasting time and money training men who aren't going through with this thing. It's perfectly all right for any of you to drop out." The colonel spoke in a casual tone, nothing tense in his voice or actions. But his manner was deceptive. He was deadly serious.

One navigator asked Doolittle if he could hand out any information about the operation.

"No, I can't—just now," the colonel said. "But you'll begin to get an idea of what it's all about the longer we're down here training for it." He went on to emphasize security. If any aviator guessed what they were going to do, he was to keep it to himself and not discuss it with his wife, his friends, or his crew. Many lives, including their own, depended upon secrecy.

Ross Greening hollered out that he'd seen some 500-foot runways chalked out on the flying field.

Doolittle said that they were there for a purpose—short, quick take-offs.

The colonel scheduled a 55-hour plan of training putting first things first. Fog and bad weather made flying impossible for days at a stretch. Hours were lost in completing installations and getting the planes operational. Training proceeded at a rapid clip, but Doolittle's schedule had to be revised downward. Only his decision to give short take-offs priority enabled every pilot to qualify.

On 2 March, Lieutenant Henry Miller, USN, reported to Eglin Field from the Naval Air Station, Pensacola. The Navy pilot had no experience with tri-cycle landing gears and could not give much instruction on actual technique, yet his advice on carrier take-offs—"drop the landing flaps and pour on the coal"—helped the pilots. On the auxiliary field's runways, Miller set up flags, one marking the starting position, the next 450 feet down the runway, and every 50 feet thereafter up to 800 feet. Men painted parallel lines 50 feet apart down the field to aid pilots in keeping the ships straight during the take-off rolls.

Each pilot reported in his own plane, and Captain Davey Jones, acting as instructor, climbed in with the ship's pilot, riding as co-pilot. At the starting line the trainee, on a nod from Jones, snapped the energizer switch to the right, primed the right engine and, after 20 seconds, flicked the toggle switch to "start" position. The right engine caught. After a similar procedure, the left engine coughed. The two engines were warming up.

Jones put the flaps down full, pushed the power controls to the full forward position with the brakes firm on, then quickly released the brakes. The plane lurched forward, then streaked, then lifted sharply into the air before it had used up 800 feet.

After the plane took off, circled the field, landed, and taxied to the starting line, Jones traded seats and rode as check pilot. They repeated the ritual.

Lieutenant Miller measured and timed each start, making the results known, watching as each pilot made three more runs down the field. After each touch down, the aviator stopped the engines, taxied back, and Miller then spelled out what was right, and what was wrong. After a little practice, ground observers could detect almost exactly what the pilot was doing in the cockpit—lifting the nose too soon or not soon enough; getting the tail too low; not pulling back hard enough on the column to lift the plane off; not rolling the stabilizer forward soon enough.

During the first phase of training, pilots flew planes lightly loaded. When each airman became proficient in "take-off" procedures, he reported with a full load of 29,000 lbs., hurtling down the runway three times. Jones and Miller watched and criticised. During the final stage, maintenance men piled in 500-lb. practice bombs, gas, ammunition until the ship weighed 31,000 lbs., and each aviator made two practice runs at this weight.

The shortest take-off was accomplished with flaps full down, stabilizer set at three-fourths, and tail heavy with full power against the brakes, which were released simultaneously as the engines came up to revs. The control column was pulled back gradually, and the plane left the ground with the tail skid about one foot from the runway.

Such techniques were contrary to everything the pilots had been taught in flight training. They sweated each run. Such lift-offs were, as one pilot put it, "inducive to a short life."

One flyboy thundering past the flags sideslipped back into the ground. He crawled away unscathed from his irreparably-damaged ship. Another bomber was lost to the mission when it developed a front wheel shimmy so violent that as the aircraft taxied it pitched forward on its nose. Time was too short to repair the slight damage.

"What'll we go in at, Colonel?" asked a pilot at Eglin.

"Fifteen hundred feet," Doolittle retorted.

This underscored to the crews the hazard of the operation, but at night they were too dog-tired to worry and from 0700 hours until 2000 hours, too busy to give danger a thought. The 24 crews were gradually learning to work together. Their take-offs grew shorter and shorter.

By the end of the quick take-off practice, which ran concurrently with other training, all pilots were extremely confident that with a 30-mile wind they could take off from a 500-foot runway. Miller marked down every trial run, and his careful records were responsible for selecting from the 24 the 16 pilots destined for Japan.

It was 1600 hours at Pearl Harbor. Vice Admiral William F. Halsey, just back from carrier strikes against Kwajalein and Marcus, was in the headquarters of Admiral Chester W. Nimitz, Commander-in-Chief, Pacific Fleet—known as CINCPAC in the Navy's jargon of endless initials. The whole war was spread out on global maps. Halsey was conferring with Duncan. The captain relayed the information that Colonel Doolittle with Navy co-operation was training Army Air Corps personnel to take B-25s off a carrier's deck. He briefed Halsey. Even if the bombers didn't inflict heavy damage, Duncan went on, they would certainly give the Japanese something to think about.

Admiral Nimitz turned to Halsey and questioned, "Do you believe it will work, Bill?"

"They'll need a lot of luck," Halsey replied.

"Are you willing to take them out there?"

"Yes, I am."

"Good," Nimitz said, "It's all yours!"

The B-25s swept in over the Florida coast and fanned out as they would do over Japan. Exact similar geographical distances were flown overland toward objectives resembling the targets in Tokyo. Doolittle ordered special training in cross-country flying, navigation, and night flying. In their legalized buzzing, pilots zipped across the countryside, their propellers inches off the ground, gaining altitude to clear houses, diving beneath telephone wires.

On these dry runs, planes barreled across the wastelands until they reached the fenced-off and restricted bombing range. Each crew unloaded 12 100-lb. practice bombs from 10,000 feet. After that, they trained at 1500 feet or less, the bombardiers adjusting their Mark Twain bombsights. Once the crews mastered the low-level runs, the pilots practiced approaches at minimum altitude with quick pull-ups to 1500 feet just before reaching the target. As each ship shot up, the bombardier opened the bomb-bay doors, made his run, released, and closed the doors. As soon as the bombs dropped, the red light winked in the cockpit for the pilot to shove the controls forward and sink to roof-top level for withdrawal. On two occasions, the commanding officer at Eglin Field detailed six P-36s and one P-40 to work with the group. The pursuits peeled off and attacked the bombers in mock battle.

Sandwiched in between take-offs and bomb training,

officers carried on ground instruction. Lieutenant Miller lectured on carrier operations and customs; navigators reviewed celestial navigation and learned to work the bombsight; all pilots not qualified in dead reckoning brushed up in abbreviated courses; and Lieutenant Thomas R. White, M.D., reviewed first-aid procedures and advised crews on what to expect in the way of diseases.

Doc White immunized the men. He brought up to date typhoid, tetanus, smallpox, and yellow fever shots, and plunged the needle into the anatomy of all airmen for typhus, cholera, bubonic plague, and pneumonia. One sore-armed sergeant, irritated and upset, groaned that if he was shot in action, he'd bleed serum.

White checked and rechecked blood typing, recorded it on the crews' dog tags, assembled first-aid kits. There were two for each plane, containing morphine syrettes, sulfa tablets, whiskey, prophylactics. Each airmen was issued a pocket-sized kit of dressings, morphine, sulfa, quinine, and iodine. Weight limitations on the plane limited White to only a medical officer's field kit plus supplies of sulfa tablets, a pocket surgical knife, and two metal catheters.

The shortage of time limited the training schedule. Few gunners were qualified for the mission. Work on the turrets so delayed gunnery practice that the men had no chance to get the feel of their weapons. Firing was so erratic that on one occasion they almost gunned down the commanding officer of Eglin. Days were lost while armament specialists wrestled and sweated under the Florida sun. Most of the gunners ground-fired their weapons on the range, bore-sighted them, and triggered a few bursts in the air, but none opened up on a towed target. Armorers completed overhauling the turrets in time so gunners could practice handling them in the air, simulating firing on other planes.

Watch-dogging his own timetable, Doolittle drove himself, the pilots, co-pilots, navigators, bombardiers, and gunners. He commuted almost daily between Eglin Field and Washington, not trusting the telephone to discuss problems with Hap Arnold at the Pentagon. Evaluating the combat crews, Doolittle concluded that the pilots were excellent; the co-pilots, good for co-pilots; the navigators had little practical experience; the gunners, still less experience.

In a quiet, downtown San Francisco restaurant, Admiral Halsey awaited his guest. As Doolittle strode in, Halsey greeted him with a wide grin. They shook hands, sat down, and started off the evening by having drinks, then ordered dinner. The booths on both sides were empty. When they finished their dessert, and more coffee arrived, Halsey waved the waiter away, and the two men got down to business.

The admiral reported that his task force consisted of two carriers, two heavy cruisers, two light cruisers, eight destroyers, two tankers. The B-25s would be loaded on board the *Hornet* in San Francisco and, escorted by half the task force, to rendezvous in mid-Pacific with the *Enterprise* and the remaining ships. If they escaped detection by the enemy, the carriers, said Halsey, would take the planes to within 400 miles of the Japanese coast. Doolittle grinned, satisfied.

Crews at Eglin Field had had four weeks of training. Bomb training. Low-level bombing, rooftop bombing. Navigation training. Dead-reckoning, celestial. Short field take-off training. Shorter take-off training, 800 feet, 500 feet. Ground school for everything—gunnery, maintenance, first aid, aircraft recognition, security.

Four weeks of it. Four weeks of striving, of tension building in an unnatural climate, part anxiety, part anticipation, part just plain excitement.

Four weeks of rumors—Tokyo, Berlin, a sub base in the Caribbean—and speculation and hunches.

Four supercharged weeks.

Without warning, the training ended.

The United States needed Generalissimo Chiang Kai-shek's approval before American bombers could touch down in Free China. The fall of Singapore had freed Japanese units for offensive thrusts against Burma. In late February, just as the first crews were reporting to Eglin Field for training, a Japanese attack fell with full force against the British lines along the Salween River, and, on 10 March, Tommies fired and evacuated Rangoon. The enemy severed the Burma Road at its base and neutralized the chief route of military supplies into China.

Drawn up in southern Yunnan Province, Chinese soldiers sweated out marching orders. The ill-starred campaign to salvage upper Burma followed. General Joseph W. Stilwell, USA, chief of the American forces in the China-India-Burma theater, took command of the Chinese force as it moved southward against the Japanese advance along the valley of the Sittang River. Preoccupied with the effort to save his command, Vinegar Joe pleaded with the Generalissimo to persuade his Chinese subordinates to recognize Stilwell's authority.

The Chinese and British soldiers, the latter retreating along the valley of the Irrawaddy River in Burma, roughly paralleling the Sittang, made a last-ditch attempt to combine in an offensive against the enemy trudging northward from Rangoon. This withered, and with it the defense of Burma deteriorated into a rear-guard action.

While the Generalissimo and Stilwell were deeply involved in the campaign to save Mandalay and Lashio, Washington sought their co-operation to establish installations at five Chinese airfields. Cablegrams to Chungking alerted the China-India-Burma command to prepare for the B-25s' reception. Chungking first learned of Special Bombing Project No. 1 through a series of requests that stores of aviation gasoline then in India be ferried into China and distributed to the fields at Kweilin, Kian, Yushan, Chuchow, and Lishui. These stocks never reached their destination.

The mission was so secret that Stilwell and Chiang Kaishek were informed on just the essentials. Washington withheld the exact character and the strategic purpose of the project. Ultimately the United States agreed to refuel the bombers with Chinese gasoline already on the ground. The hesitant Generalissimo, desperate for air support, gave his blessing to the mission on 28 March.

Shortly after 1300 hours that afternoon, the submarine, *Thresher,* took departure from Midway Island. The operation had begun.

On the same day, maintenance men at McClellan Field in Sacramento, California, slaved over the stripped-down B-25s with their cheaply-made bombsights, rubber-bag gas tanks, and phoney wooden tail guns. The bomber crews, rested after their low-altitude flight from Eglin, supervised last minute check-outs. All B-25s were equipped with new three-bladed propellers. "I want every first pilot to make absolutely certain," Doolittle explained, "that his plane is in perfect shape, and that his crew also is."

The Doolittle contingent was irritated by the complacency of the officers and men attached to McClellan Field. Mechanics revved the engines so fast that the new propeller blades swooped up dirt, pockmarking their tips. Ski York was angry when ground crews goofed up and changed the carburetor on his plane. This obviously affected the fuel consumption of his engines, yet he had no time to make another cross-country test run. Doc White chewed out an unco-operative medical supply officer who, unwilling to deplete his stores, alibied and refused to fill requisitions.

Security prevented Doolittle's crews from fraternizing with their counterparts at McClellan—a careless word, an off-chance remark might reveal sensitive information. They stuck together, declining to drink at the Officers' Club, and were labeled "a bunch of stuck-up s.o.b.'s."

Simultaneously with their arrival at McClellan Field, Captain Duncan, unwilling to trust details to paper, flew to San Diego from Pearl Harbor to discuss with Captain Marc "Pete" Mitscher, USN, of the *Hornet,* the carrier's departure. They worked out the time and the latitude and longitude for the *Hornet*'s rendezvous in the Pacific with the other half of the task force, which would sail from Pearl. Duncan requested that Mitscher get under way from San Diego and steam northward to San Francisco to load Doolittle's planes and men.

Shortly after the *Hornet* docked at Alameda Naval Air Station, Lieutenant John F. Sutherland, USN, and other naval aviators watched a bunch of B-25s roar in low over the ship and land at a nearby field. Sutherland and his friends jeered at the Army pilots' techniques and jested that those junior birdmen were standing in the need of naval indoctrination. Flights of bombers were no novelty, and these aroused little interest among the sailors until the following day, when the airdales turned to in full force to clear the flight deck and store the *Hornet's* own planes below.

The carrier's deck lay bare in the sun on 1 April. Army donkeys towed 16 B-25s down the dock where cranes hooked them up and gently placed them on the *Hornet's* flight deck. Navy personnel blocked their wheels and lashed them down. The bombers looked alien and awkward to the airdales. Curiosity grew acute when, in the afternoon, khaki-clad flyboys appeared at the gangway.

Naval aviators squinted up at the hulking planes scattered across the flight deck. Army pilots led guided tours through the bombers, bragging about their air speed and range. Not to be outdone, the Navy followed by the Army clambered below decks and inspected the Wildcats and Devastators, with wings folded, and dismantled SBDs, which were packed into every available space, even hung from the overhead.

Corporal Larry Bogart, United States Marines, Mitscher's orderly, stood at rigid attention outside the captain's cabin, where he heard the preliminary greetings. Some officer said, "Lieutenant Colonel Doolittle, Captain." Bogart kept his station. The *Hornet's* executive officer said, "Hello Jimmy." Suddenly, Bogart knew. This was Jimmy Doolittle, the famous pilot, the guy with all the flight records. The corporal cocked his ear to catch the rest of the conversation. He didn't.

Below in the crews' quarters, scuttlebutt spread. The *Hornet* was going to reinforce Hawaii. She was going to the Dutch East Indies. She was going to the Indian Ocean. She was going to Alaskan waters. She was going to New Zealand. She was going south. She was going north.

In his office on board, Sergeant George Royce, United

States Marines, called his men together. He hadn't the faintest idea what was up, but he suggested to his detachment that any who had failed to take out Government Life Insurance would be wise to do so immediately. Three took his advice. Corporal Bogart increased his from $1000 to $5000.

On the dock, a representative of an aircraft company heard that the *Hornet* was delivering 16 bombers to Honolulu. Transportation was scarce. He had important business in Hawaii. Threatening to pull wires in Washington, he insisted on a free ride. He was adamant. The Navy gave in.

While Doolittle and Mitscher conferred on board the *Hornet,* Washington was cabling additional instructions to Chungking as to arrangements and services. The airfields were ordered to be in readiness on the night of 19–20 April. This dispatch included a warning that the arrival of the B-25s might be changed without notice.

On that same day, an Army officer climbed into a plane at Karachi, India, headed for Chungking, from where he was to proceed by air to the five Chinese airports to inspect the facilities and instruct native personnel in radio, emergency channels, and signals.

On the afternoon of 1 April, the *Hornet* nosed out of her berth at Alameda Naval Air Station and dropped anchor in San Francisco Bay, her flight deck jammed with bombers exposed to unfriendly observation. But the speed and urgency of the mission left no time for camouflage. Airdales had parked the planes in their take-off positions. Several of Doolittle's pilots questioned such procedures. They argued that *Hornet* personnel should have spread the B-25s over the whole flight deck to give the impression that they would be hoisted off at a destination rather than be flown.

That evening Corporal Dave Thatcher stayed on board the carrier; Lieutenant Frank Kappeler visited his home in Alameda. The majority of the airmen and sailors went ashore in San Francisco for one last fling.

At the *Chronicle* offices, Navy commanders McConnell and Abernathy, just back from the war zone, told newsmen of their experiences when the seaplane tender, *Langley,* and the tanker, *Pecos,* went down in the Indian Ocean south of Java, bombarded by Japanese planes. In another part of San Francisco, on Post Street from Octavia to Fillmore, 660 Japanese-Americans were packing up, ready to leave for the duration in the Army's first forced evacuation affecting northern California. Houseboys, lawyers, doctors, gardeners, laundrymen, and fisherfolk were destined for Santa Anita Race Track in Arcadia. In front of their stores hung posters, "Evacuation Sale."

The sailors and airmen surged up Market Street. A few raced through the city rubbernecking, taking a drink here and there along the way. They saw the ferry tower and the buildings on Nob Hill. A couple of enlisted men went to the Golden Gate Theater to see the movie, "Joan of Paris," with singing star Dick Powell and Jack Teagarden's orchestra on stage. Others congregated at the Liberty Follies at Broadway near Stockton to ogle the strippers and savor Ann Corio in the movie, "Swamp Woman." At John's Grill, a San Francisco businessman bet six officers $100 each that the war would be over in 1943. In the gin mills, the tired sopranos groaned out "Deep in the Heart of Texas" and invited the bored audiences to join in on the clapping. "I remember lots of things about San Francisco that night," recalled a pilot, "but they're not for publication."

Officers started for the St. Francis Hotel, and they collected others on the way. They discovered the Mural Room closed, but learned that Harry Owens and his Royal Hawaiians would open next week. They stormed up the hill to the Mark Hopkins, teamed up with friends, and worked their way up to the "Top of the Mark." To the tinkle of glasses and the music of "Sleepy Lagoon," they gazed out at the harbor.

It was fine to sit there and look out on San Francisco below, at the bay and at the *Hornet.* They felt lighthearted, adventuresome, fine, and this night was going to be a lulu—it had to be—because it was the last one stateside.

———

At 1000 hours, 2 April 1942, the *Hornet,* heavy cruiser *Vincennes,* light cruiser *Nashville,* the oiler *Cimarron,* and the destroyers *Gwin, Grayson, Meredith,* and *Monssen*—Task Group 16.2—stood down San Francisco Bay in heavy fog. A fast-moving Navy gig darted from a dock to catch up with the *Hornet.* Doolittle was wanted on shore. General George C. Marshall, Army Chief of Staff, was on the telephone from the Pentagon. The colonel went down the gangway to the waiting gig.

He picked up the phone.

"Doolittle?" Marshall asked.

"Yes, General."

"I couldn't let you leave without wishing you the best of luck. Our hearts will be with you and our prayers will be with you. Good-bye, and good luck and come back safely."

"Thank you," Doolittle replied. He put down the receiver.

Task Group 16.2 passed under the Golden Gate Bridge at 1130 hours and, at 1327 hours, set course 294°, speed

16 knots. Shortly after a Navy blimp dropped two boxes of the navigator's domes on the *Hornet*'s deck, the boatswain's pipe shrilled over the bull horns. The executive officer bellowed, "Now hear this." Men listened to the captain's voice. The carrier was headed into Japanese waters, perhaps to within 400 miles of Tokyo, to launch the B-25s. Pete Mitscher warned the crew to throw nothing overboard that identified the ship—no letters, no magazines, no newspapers. The bull horn clicked off. Now all hands shared the secret.

Cheers thundered throughout the ship. The face of the aircraft company's representative turned ashen when he realized he was on an extended cruise. Birdmen and bluejackets pounded each other on the back, whooping and hollering, delirious that they were helping to deliver a blow against Japan proper. A gay little song swept through the carrier, to the tune from "Snow White," "Hiho, hi-ho, we're off to Tokyo! We'll bomb and blast and come back fast."

Beneath the hilarity and horseplay there was a tenseness. Officers felt it in the wardroom, seamen felt it in the crews' quarters, in the carpenter's shop, in the lookouts, on the bridge. The *Hornet*'s dive bombers, fighters, and scouts on which she depended for reconnaissance and protection were stowed below. Except for an occasional observation plane catapulted from the cruisers, the carrier was blind. Helpless to defend herself if intercepted by Japanese planes or surface craft, she had to rely on the guns of the escorts. How near to Japan dared the *Hornet* steam?

Mitscher's signalmen semaphored their destination to the escorting vessels. On board the tanker *Cimarron*, Commander Russell H. Ihrig, USN, switched on the loudspeakers and delivered a "War Message to All Hands."

"If you expect to survive in enemy waters," he said, "you will have to do your best. Don't think of the Japs as far away. They have already been to Pearl Harbor! THINK OF THEM AS HERE."

Deck gangs on the tanker turned out early that afternoon, scrubbing down all deck surfaces with warm water and soap, dumping overboard rubber matting, distributing flashlights and battle lanterns throughout the ship, in magazines, in dressing stations, in pump rooms, in the after engineering spaces. Officers checked life jackets and warned seamen to don full winter underwear as flash protection.

"This new assignment," Ihrig told his officers, "will probably place us under fire, not only from subs, but from aircraft and surface ships. Be fully prepared to go into action TO WIN."

"Remember," he finished, "there is *no second place* in a sea fight. Do your thinking *now* and ACT IN ACTION. Only hard work will win this war. THERE IS A JOB TO BE DONE, GO TO IT. AND REMEMBER PEARL HARBOR!"

The ship's barber clipped the men's hair short. Officers readied their staterooms as dressing stations. The gunnery officer mounted all .30-caliber machine guns and inspected the tracer assemblies on all .50-caliber ready ammunition. The first lieutenant unhinged all inner non-watertight doors and carried away all curtains, including shower curtains, except those necessary for the blackout. The construction and repair gang stowed sledges, hammers, heavy bars at all watertight doors to aid in opening them quickly if jammed. They wiped down all bulkheads, light fixtures, furniture, overheads of pipes, and wiring to clear the tanker of dust. Men shaved off beards, washed their heads clean of tonic, and threw overboard shoe polish and hair oils. To guard against flying fragments, seamen unscrewed and secured all curtain rods, clothes hooks, port hooks, small metal cabinets and shelves, shower soap holders.

Task Group 16.2 plowed westward in foul weather, encountering howling winds, heavy seas, frequent rain, and squalls. Personnel constantly inspected the B-25s, making sure they were lashed tight to the flight deck. The *Hornet*'s aviation machinists and Army personnel checked out minor difficulties—generator failures, bad spark plugs, leaky gas tanks, brakes. On one occasion, they yanked the engine from a plane, repaired it below in the carrier's shops, and reinstalled it.

Heavy swells made refueling at sea hazardous and called for a high order of seamanship. On the *Cimarron*, pitching violently, seaman first class P. D. Williams slipped and plunged overboard. Rocketing through the surging sea, the destroyer, *Meredith*, hauled him in uninjured.

Doolittle called his men into an empty wardroom to give them the Big Picture. Ten thousand men, perhaps more, had contributed to the organization of the Tokyo operation. Top brass in the Navy and Army, personnel at Wright Field, at Eglin, at McClellan, at Alameda had helped. Naval officers, CPOs, and seamen were presently executing their part in the intricate and interlocked pattern which Captain Duncan had so brilliantly designed. As the colonel spoke, only seven beside himself understood the complete operation—King, Duncan, Nimitz, Halsey, Mitscher, Arnold, and Low.

The targets were Tokyo, Yokohama, Osaka, Kobe, Nagoya. The Navy would haul them in close to the Japanese coast to launch the B-25s. Mileage? Gas consumption? Course? It was going to be a tight squeeze, Doolittle warned. The Generalissimo was co-operating and, after hitting the targets, they were to land at airfields not far inland from the coast, gas up, and fly on to Chungking.

Doolittle continued. News had arrived that the Russians had turned down the American request to land at Vladivostok. Those fields were out. Under no circumstances were the crews to head for Russia. If the task force were attacked at sea the planes would take off immediately and make for Hawaii or Midway. If there was no time to launch, the fliers were to jettison the bombers into the sea so the *Hornet* could send up her own fighters. The colonel impressed upon them that the Navy was in command until the B-25s were airborne. This was to be no suicide mission. Doolittle's calculations gave every man at least a 50-50 chance.

The briefing over, the crews wandered out toward their bombers. Pilots walked nervously down the flight deck, pacing off the take-off distance. It was damned short. Lieutenant Ted Lawson handed out paper pads to his men and urged them to list everything that came into their heads which would put their aircraft in better condition.

Captain Pete Mitscher had vacated his elaborate stateroom for Doolittle and moved to an emergency cabin on the bridge.

Most of the Army officers were either quartered in captain's country in cots or bunked with naval aviators in their staterooms; enlisted men shared the CPOs' quarters, where Sergeant Jacob Eierman reported the food to be "swell."

The crew of the *Hornet* and the Navy pilots on board respected these Army flyboys destined for Tokyo. From Mitscher down to the galley boys, they did everything to ease pressures and make life pleasant for the raiders. Sailors lent soldiers clothing while theirs was at the laundry. Mechanics shared tools and time. Enlisted Army personnel had not been paid since the days at Eglin Field. Waving regulations aside, Mitscher ordered the supply officer to pay them from Navy funds.

It was open house day and night at the galley and bake shop. The cooks and stewards dished up three meals per day and attempted to feed officers and men every time they were hungry. Bakers mixed up extra cakes, cookies, and pies.

Many a sailor went off with a piece of pie in one hand, a roast beef sandwich in the other, directly into the mess line to draw his ration.

Inveterate coffee drinkers, crews gulped down coffee 24 hours a day. Urns were never empty. The men set up some 50-odd coffee messes with their own percolators and, drawing the dry coffee issued free, brewed and drank their own joe.

On a typical day at sea, bomber crews climbed out of their cots when they felt like it and breakfasted around 0800 hours. They went out on deck to examine their planes, warmed them up, adjusted, and poked through the equipment. From their top turrets, gunners fired short bursts at kites; navigators shot the stars and sun, computed the carrier's position, and checked these findings with the *Hornet*'s officers.

Every day, combat crews filed into the wardroom for skull practice—lectures on plane maintenance, lectures on gunnery, lectures on bombardment, lectures on first aid. Quietly, precisely, Doolittle in one of these sessions hashed over the schedule, turning to the chart tacked to the bulkhead—launch on 19 April, bomb Tokyo, escape into Free China. No papers, no notes were to be taken along which might disclose the planes' origin, their proposed path, their destination. After each aircraft took off, Doolittle emphasized, each member of each crew would be responsible for his own personal safety, for the safety of the plane, and for the successful fulfillment of the mission.

Lieutenant Stephen Jurika, Jr., USN, once naval attache in Japan and a treasure-house of information, gave it to the fliers straight, without exaggerating or minimizing. He drummed into the crews the Chinese phrase, *Lushu hoo megwa fugi* ("I am an American") and briefed them on ways to tell a Chinese from a Japanese, the enemy's industrial setup, Tokyo, the terrain, construction and the value of the targets. Bombers were to avoid all stone, concrete, and steel targets as their bomb loads were insufficient to damage these.

⌜Tokyo, Yokohama, Nagoya, Osaka, and Kobe were major centers of the Japanese war effort. The target areas afforded the bombardiers every type of military objective—harbor facilities, shipbuilding yards, heavy machine plants, steel mills, communication and transportation centers. All these cities were exceptionally vulnerable to incendiary bombs. In Tokyo alone there were 1,029,695 buildings and dwellings, the majority of which were flimsy wood and bamboo.⌟

The bombing problems were complicated. Doolittle instructed each crew to unload its four bombs where they would inflict the most damage and to release them in the shortest possible time while flying a straight line. Such tactics exposed the B-25s to the minimum amount of antiaircraft fire.

Airmen studied cities and geographical landmarks from blown-up aerial photographs and huge target maps. These charts contained only the numbered targets, covered a small area, and were detailed to show highways, railroad tracks, the terrain, pinpointing dwelling houses and all buildings. The layouts became indelible in the crews' minds. Each pilot, co-pilot, bombardier, navigator, and gunner memorized his objectives. All non-military facilities were to be avoided. To hit hospitals, schools, and residential areas would be to waste bombs, cause unnecessary civilian casualties, and create useless enmity against American prisoners of war.

When one session ended, fliers cut cards for the right to bomb the Imperial Palace and Emperor Hirohito. The colonel, hearing the ruckus, ate them out and ordered them to leave the Palace absolutely alone, to pound nothing but military objectives.

Studying the layouts, Doolittle decided to employ 13 planes against the Tokyo-Yokohama area, and drop only incendiary bombs on the other cities. Each element of three planes was given a sector to strike: Doolittle, flying unattached, Shiba Ward; Lieutenant Travis Hoover, commanding the first element, northern Tokyo; Captain Davey Jones, second element, business district north of the Imperial Palace; Captain Ski York, third element, the area from Shiba Ward west to Yokohama; Captain Ross Greening, fourth element, Yokohama with one plane on the Yokohama Navy Yard; Major Jack Hilger, fifth element, one bomber each to Nagoya, Kobe, Osaka.

Within these sectors, each element leader assigned the individual B-25s to definite, carefully selected targets. The choice of objective, route, and method of approach was discussed and co-ordinated with the colonel.

From Army and Navy intelligence sources, crews were informed that over 500 combat planes were in Japan, most of them concentrated in the Tokyo area. Bomber pilots, operating in the Far Eastern Theater after 7 December, had emphasized to intelligence officers that enemy fighters employed varied tactics when attacking. Usually they flew in a three-plane, loose V formation, approaching out of the bomber's gun range, breaking off individually, hitting simultaneously from the rear quarter, from above, and from below. Enemy pursuits opened fire at short range.

Despite the lectures, briefings, confabs, check-out lists, many crew members confessed, later, that more attention should have been directed to emergency take-off procedures and escape and evasion techniques in enemy-held territory.

The Navy and Air Corps had agreed that the planes would take off immediately after contact was made with enemy patrol vessels, no matter what latitude or longitude. Doolittle and his staff considered a dawn attack. A take-off about three hours before daylight would give the greatest security, provide ideal bombing conditions, assure surprise, and permit arrival at the Chinese bases before dark. They scrapped this idea. A night launch was too hazardous, and the Navy refused to light up the flight deck in enemy waters.

Another plan was to launch at dawn, hit Tokyo in the early morning, fly to Free China, and land before nightfall. But daylight bombing increased the danger of accurate antiaircraft opposition and interception by enemy pursuits.

Carefully and precisely computing the risk of meeting Japanese surface vessels or planes, Doolittle adopted a third plan, a night attack to be launched at dusk, 19 April. The bombers would unload their eggs at night, withdrawing and touching down at their destination after daylight, 20 April. To insure success, one plane, Doolittle's, was to take off ahead of schedule, fly over the objectives just before dark, firing the most inflammable part of the city, lighting up Tokyo to guide the other aircraft. The pilots disapproved vehemently of

Doolittle's run three hours before dark—it was too risky and would force him to land in China at night. Discounting their objections, the colonel held to this operation.

What action should they take in case of engine or aircraft failure over Japanese-held territory? Doolittle gave each and every man a free hand. Personally, he said, he did not intend to be taken prisoner and that, if his plane was crippled beyond any possibility of escape, he'd dive it at full throttle into whatever target lay below him. He added that he was 46, had lived a full life, and was in no position to dictate to the other pilots, most of whom were in their early 20s. He left this decision to the judgment of each plane captain.

The success of the raid depended upon the carrier closing the gap between herself and Japan. If the planes were launched within 450 miles of the coast, the gamble was excellent. At 550 miles, the odds were slight. Six hundred and fifty miles was the absolute outside limit, a hell of a chance.

To relax from the arduous training schedule, Corporal Dave Thatcher rummaged through the ship, fascinated by the throbbing engines. Lieutenant Dick Cole tinkered in the machine shop, fashioning a new screw for the hinge of his sunglasses. Doc White jotted notes in his journal. Corporal Jacob DeShazer lazily watched the dancing porpoises alongside. In the evening, after a stop at the "gedunk" wagon, a few applauded and whistled at the movies.

The majority gambled—poker, acey deucey, craps, darts. Captain Mitscher came in one evening and stood behind a second lieutenant, who was concentrating on the poker game, a cigar stuck in his mouth. "How are you doing?" inquired the captain.

Hardly glancing up, the flyboy replied, "O.K., Joe, want to take a hand?" much to the embarrassment of the marine corporal standing behind the captain.

The crews played with fierce intensity. Stakes climbed until a single pot contained a month's pay. The airmen took the Navy for every dollar they had, but, as the voyage wore on, they lost it all, and more.

Gambling, confessed Lieutenant Commander William J. "Gus" Widhelm, wasn't really his fault. He'd prefer to loaf in his cabin and listen to his Bing Crosby records or his Harry James and Guy Lombardo collections, but swarms of music lovers, congregating in his room, drove him to the poker tables. He played regularly, night and day, and when he waved the Army off for Tokyo, he was $1,100 richer.

Little gusts of wind stirred the beaches, but the sun poked through the clouds often enough to make the day warm. It was mid-morning, 8 April, in Honolulu. Hawaiians were depressed by the war news.

In the Philippines the defense line on Bataan had collapsed, and American survivors were retreating to Corregidor. The Solomon Islands had been overrun. Japanese troops occupied Rangoon, the key to lower Burma. The Rising Sun flew over the Andaman Islands, islands which put the enemy in a position to strike India.

To secure the sea route to Burma, Admiral Nagumo's units steamed into the Indian Ocean. On Easter Sunday, 5 April, his carrier planes hit the British base at Colombo, Ceylon, and, afterwards, sent the British heavy cruisers, *Dorsetshire* and *Cornwall*, to the bottom. Four days later Nagumo's planes struck Trincomalee, the other British base in Ceylon. That same afternoon, the enemy sank the carrier, *Hermes,* and an escorting destroyer.

Vice Admiral Takeo Kurita, meanwhile, was entering the Bay of Bengal with heavy cruisers and a light carrier. In nine days, Japanese air, surface, and submarine units destroyed four British warships and 135,000 tons of merchant shipping.

After this blitz, the British all but pulled out of the Indian Ocean. A Japanese invasion of Ceylon and India seemed imminent. Prime Minister Winston Churchill in London urged that the United States Navy take offensive measures to force the enemy to draw their units back into the Pacific.

By coincidence, at Ford Island, Pearl Harbor, the aircraft carrier *Enterprise,* flying the flag of Vice Admiral Halsey, was getting under way at 1120 hours, 8 April. She threaded her way down channel together with the cruisers *Northampton* and *Salt Lake City,* the destroyers *Balch, Benham,* and *Fanning* and, once at sea, rendezvoused with the destroyer *Ellet* and the oiler *Sabine.* The last units of the expedition for Tokyo had taken departure. Task Group 16.1 steamed on a course to a point 30 miles southwest of Nihoa Island in the Hawaiian group. From there the ships shifted course to 310°, the *Enterprise* maintaining continuous inner and intermediate air patrols during the daylight hours, weather permitting.

From 2 April until the 10th, Chungking and Washington had exchanged messages looking toward the establishment of radio equipment at the key airfields. In the time remaining, the American officer from Karachi would visit the fields and alert personnel directly concerned with the operation. Nothing could be entrusted to the haphazard Chinese communications. The fields were all within 1000 miles of Chungking so that, on the surface, the problem appeared not too difficult. But a protracted period of bad weather was beginning to break over eastern China, threatening the entire Tokyo project.

Suddenly, without warning, Washington received a disheartening shock. Chiang Kai-shek demanded that the raid be postponed until late May. He argued that the planes be diverted against enemy bases in Burma and naval craft in the Bay of Bengal. In an acrimonious exchange, Washington advised that the operation could not be recalled or changed. Radio silence prevented warning the *Hornet* of the crisis.

The principal Japanese island of Honshu, towards which the *Hornet* headed, bends westward in its lower half toward the mainland of Asia; the upper portion runs north and south. Where the coastline changes direction lies the Boso Peninsula, covering the entrance of Tokyo Bay. The easternmost projection of this body of land is Inubo Saki (Cape), which is the part of Japan nearest Hawaii and the natural landfall of ships or planes approaching from that direction.

The submarine *Thresher* was preparing to round O Shima to the north and proceed down channel to Inubo Saki. At 0751 hours, Commander Anderson cushioned one eye against the rubber-cupped eye piece and turned the periscope around. A 10,000-ton freighter was heading his way. At 0806, 0808, 0810 hours Anderson fired torpedoes. They missed. Two hours later, through the periscope, the *Thresher* spotted a 5000-ton cargo ship steaming southward. One torpedo blasted into her. She crumpled at her center, bow and stern up, and went down in less than three minutes.

A Japanese sub chaser, eager for the kill, unleashed a merciless depth charge attack. The reports were deafening. The *Thresher* trembled. The attack ceased. Just as the *Thresher* was surfacing, Commander Anderson picked up a supersonic echo and started maneuvers to evade. In the cramped innards of the submarine, the crew heard the engines of the sub chasers, looking here, looking there, searching. Depth charges. *Boom. Boom. Boom. Boom,* continuously, rapidly for fifteen minutes. Relentless. This time they were very close. The blue-jackets heard a rumble in the sub's propellers and a pronounced rattle coming from the superstructure over the wardroom. The racket grew louder, guiding the attackers to the target.

In frantic efforts to run slow, hampered by a leaky negative flood and with charges detonating all around, Anderson lost depth control momentarily. The *Thresher* descended to 400 feet before the skipper could start her up again. The attack stopped, and the submarine, leaking badly, surfaced at 2317 hours and cleared the zone.

The submarine *Trout*, on that same day in April, was patrolling two miles off Muroto Saki. Her captain, Lieutenant Commander F. W. Fenno, Jr., saw the heavy, black smoke of a steamer at 1158 hours. One torpedo slithered down the tubes. It missed. The enemy heeled over to starboard, turning toward the submarine at a rapid rate, enveloped in a smoke screen. The sub chaser shot out from behind the smudge and bolted for the *Trout*. In a split second Fenno decided to send one more torpedo at the freighter. It missed. Now both vessels bore in on the *Trout*. Fenno dove her deep, believing that they had run into a Japanese "Q" ship or decoy. The sub chaser dumped no charges. The *Trout* fled the area.

Early the next morning a torpedo from the *Trout* slammed into a 15,000-ton freighter, which swung to starboard, blowing her whistles frantically. The *Trout* moved in, but the cargo ship turned and headed for the beach. The next time Fenno peered through the periscope, the enemy was standing out to sea again. The *Trout* fired one more torpedo, which went wide. The vessel, slightly down by the stern, opened the range rapidly.

Commanders of both the *Trout* and *Thresher* entered in their war diaries that day the presence of many tugboat-sized patrol vessels snooping about in a relatively small area.

The sun was shining brightly in Tokyo when radio intelligence alerted the Japanese Army and Navy commands. An enemy task force, built around two or three carriers was in the vicinity of 28-00 North, 164-00 East. From the position of the ships, the high command surmised that the enemy might conduct an air raid on one of Japan's industrial centers on or about 14 April.

On 13 April, in latitude 38-00 North, longitude 180-00 West, a point between Midway and the Western Aleutians, the *Enterprise* and her escorts rendezvoused with Mitscher's Task Group 16.2. To the men on the *Hornet,* the *Enterprise* with planes packed on the flight deck, ready to battle the enemy at a moment's notice, was a welcome sight. As the two groups merged into Task Force 16, the ships maneuvered to take up station. The *Hornet,* the guide ship, was in the center, followed by the *Sabine, Cimarron,* and *Enterprise.* The cruisers and destroyers screened ahead and on the flank. The ships pounded silently on, crossing the International Date Line, losing April 14th.

Lieutenant Colonel E. H. Alexander and Major E. N. Backus left Chungking in utter secrecy to make final arrangements at the Chinese airfields to prepare them to receive the American B-25s. They were to arrange for the transmission of DF (Direction-Finding) signals and the lighting of the fields, beginning two hours before daylight on 20 April; to supply the bases with landing flares; to check on the gasoline; to insure the presence of interpreters.

Alexander and Backus flew by cargo plane to Chengtu, where they changed into two Curtiss Hawk III Chinese fighters for the trip to Kweilin, Kian, Yushan, Chuchow, Lishui. Plunging into zero-zero weather, the Chinese fighters put back to Chungking, but the entire area was socked in. At 1845 hours Alexander let down through the overcast, spied a sand bar in the Chialing River, and landed. Backus abandoned his plane by parachute. Chinese authorities hustled both officers to the nearest airport, Sui Ning, but four days had been lost. A fresh start was planned for 17 April in a DC-3.

Just as Backus was bailing out, the *Thresher* was surfacing in enemy waters, running on two engines and charging on the auxiliary. The weather was squally. Suddenly, a gigantic wave smashed over the *Thresher's* bridge. Water raced through the conning tower hatch and the engine induction before the engines could be stopped and the boat sealed. Water flooded every compartment. In the pump room bilges, sea water lapped over the deck plates. In the after battery, three inches swished over the deck. In the engine room, water was up to the main generators. Several pieces of machinery and the main cables to No. 1 main generator grounded. Two days were wasted before the damaged submarine could join the *Trout* and assume the silent watch for enemy planes and task forces.

With the *Hornet* in the western Pacific fast approaching the point of launch, Admiral King in Washington went to the White House to tell the President the complete plan. This was the first detailed information that President Roosevelt had on the raid.

On 15 April the Chungking message from Stilwell's headquarters advised Washington that the Generalissimo had again agreed to the use of all airfields except Chuchow, the major airfield close to the coast. This information could not be relayed to Doolittle.

Cut off by radio silence on the *Hornet,* Doolittle informed his men that once they had bombed the targets and had withdrawn, they were all to head for Chuchow. These were tense days on the *Hornet* and *Enterprise* as the task force sliced deeper and deeper into enemy waters, bucking strong head winds and mounting seas. Private radios registered the approach to Japan. American programs faded out, and the crews no longer heard Jack Benny, Fred Allen, and the baseball games. Fiddling with the dials of their receivers, which CPOs inspected to prevent defects from giving off telltale waves, the men picked up a jumble of Japanese propaganda programs beamed out of Tokyo in English.

Sailors and airmen were flabbergasted when Tokyo radio's broadcast of 16 April reported: "Reuter's, British News Agency, has announced that three American bombers have dropped bombs on Tokyo. This is a laughable story. They know it is absolutely impossible for enemy bombers to get within 500 miles of Tokyo. Instead of worrying about such foolish things, the Japanese people are enjoying the fine spring sunshine and the fragrance of cherry blossoms."

Airdales on the *Hornet* spotted the planes for take-off.

The lead ship, Doolittle's, had only 467 feet of clear deck and the last B-25 hung precariously out over the stern ramp. Each crew member was issued a pistol, parachute, knife, extra clips of ammunition, one day's Type C field ration, a flashlight, a full canteen of water, and a Navy gas mask. Identification tags were rechecked.

Doolittle and his staff scrutinized each bomber to see if it was in proper condition. A thorough check-off list was handed out. Each B-25 captain was held responsible to his element leader, and each element leader to Doolittle for the detailed execution of this order.

On the flight deck that afternoon, 16 April, Doolittle read to his combat crews God-speed messages from Marshall, King, and Arnold and, along with Mitscher and the airmen, posed for publicity pictures. Mitscher produced a handful of Japanese medals, which had been awarded to him and others in happier years when they were visiting Japan.

"It's time we sent these medals back where they came from," he snorted. "Suppose we tie them to the bombs you are going to drop."

Mitscher and the colonel ceremoniously attached them. Four 500-lb. demolition bombs were inscribed with "I don't want to set the world on fire—just Tokyo"; others with appropriate slogans deriding Emperor Hirohito and Premier Hideki Tojo. On one casing, Marine Corporal Bogart chalked, "This one is from Mom and Pop Bogart."

Taking off in a DC-3, Alexander and Backus started from Chungking on 17 April in a final effort to reach and supply the key airfields. This time Chinese radio operators, who were to man the communication setups, were with them in the plane. Fog and rain closed in.

The DC-3 was flying on instruments when its radio conked out. The aircraft turned back.

17 April, 1000 miles east of Tokyo. Tankers began refueling the carriers and cruisers. The weather was "the God-damnedest I've ever seen," groused Lieutenant Robin Lindsey, USN. Waves smashed over the tankers, their bows dipping down into the huge, rolling swells. The hoses were barely withdrawn before winds hit gale force.

At 1439 hours, the two carriers and four cruisers stepped out at a speed of 28 knots for the final run. The destroyers and tankers dropped astern to conserve fuel and permit high speed operations.

Soaked lookouts scanned the horizon. Whitecapped rollers burst over the bows of the cruisers. Spray leaped over the flight decks of the carriers. With the waves so high, the deck pitching so violently, a sailor tried to hold the *Enterprise*'s landing signal officer in place on the platform. As the scouting planes thundered in, the officer slipped several times and, later, he chuckled, "You can imagine the amazement on the pilot's face as he passed over with no signal officer there."

That night, 17 April, Halsey communicated with Doolittle. The task force would run all night and continue the next day until intercepted. The carriers and cruisers were nearing Japan a whole day ahead of the schedule discussed with Chungking. Doolittle was not overly disturbed. Stilwell's headquarters would pick up Tokyo Radio. The landing fields would have adequate warning.

The *Hornet* was taut. Everyone—flier and sailor alike—felt the zero hour approaching. Pilots continuously checked with Mitscher's weather prophets and studied all forecasts and maps. Tense, keyed-up men in the wardroom stared at the big chart on the bulkhead and counted the miles back to the United States. They were a long way from home. Somebody got a laugh by asking, "Anybody seen the Staten Island Ferry go by?" A dance band came in loud over a short wave radio from San Francisco, and everybody felt better. The fliers, some fully clothed, settled down to get what rest they could. No one could predict when the order would come to take off. They knew that all hell would break loose in the skies over Tokyo in a matter of hours.

In Tokyo, citizens picked up their evening newspapers. The headlines reported merciless bomber attacks against American-held Corregidor, Japanese landings at Panay, mopping-up operations on Cebu. The "dastardly British" had sunk a Japanese hospital ship.

The general election was coming up. Campaign posters adorned government offices, business firms, and department stores. Mrs. Yayoi Yoshioka was entertaining 100 women leaders to map out additional street campaigns with the help of school girls.

Bereaved families of Japanese war dead were arriving in Tokyo from all parts of the Empire to attend a special spring festival at the Yasukuni Shrine. In the parlor of the Central Hotel, Shizuko, the only daughter of the late Captain Tadao Yamamoto, commented to a reporter, "It was awfully cold last night on the train." Upstairs the widow of Captain Mitsuru Tsurunaga quietly placed baskets of bananas and oranges on the window sill, an offering to her husband's heroic spirit.

At Radio Station JOAK Mrs. Machi Ota chatted in a

motherly voice with the people of Burma. She encouraged them to resist western imperialism and to reconstruct Burma for the Burmese.

Next to the Imperial Hotel at the Takarazuka Theater, Fukuko Sayo of the Takarazuka Ballet was in her last performance of "Moontroupe." At the Hibiya Public Hall, Professor Manfred Gurlitt was conducting the Tokyo Symphony Orchestra in Beethoven's Fifth. The News Theater was featuring "Avalanche," two reels; "Bird and Rabbit," a cartoon; "Skiing Squads of the Imperial Navy," two reels; the latest films from the Bataan front.

Toshi Go of the *Japan Times and Advertiser* sat musing, preparing an editorial. "With the imminent fall of Corregidor," he wrote, "the entire waters of the southwestern Pacific will become an exclusive lake for the Japanese Navy, and all American and British warships will be completely shut out."

Preparations for the war against Great Britain and the United States had drained the resources of his country to such a point prior to the outbreak of the war that the defense of the homeland had been neglected. After the start of hostilities, the success of initial operations had lulled her into believing no full scale defensive preparations for the homeland was necessary.

Toshi Go prophesied: "With the loss of their naval bases in these parts of the world, warships of the United States and Britain have been made into inglorious, baseless vagabonds of the high seas. But fortunately the matter is much simplified as most of them already have been sent to the bottom by Japanese warships which have swept Anglo-American ships clean of these waters. All their ballyhoo about a summer offensive is the wishful thinking of desperate allied leaders."

The Army and Navy, anticipating a short war, sacrificed all the newly-activated forces, ships, aircraft, and other weapons and material for continuous offensive moves. This situation compelled Japan to neglect the defense of her home islands.

Toshi Go finished his editorial and went home.

That night Metropolitan Police visited the interned American and British embassies. Curtly they issued instructions for the next morning, Saturday, 18 April. There would be an air-raid drill throughout Tokyo.

ATTACK

IN THE *Enterprise's* RADAR SHACK, BLEARY-EYED men of the mid-watch stared at their scopes. An hour slipped by. Suddenly, at 0310 hours, 18 April, they spotted two surface craft bearing 255°. On the bridge, lookouts excitedly reported two white lights bearing the same. Instantly, on TBS orders, the task force turned sharply 90° to starboard, course 350°.

The ear-splitting *clang, clang, clang* of the general quarters startled the *Hornet*. There was a sudden rushing. Men poured down passageways, up ladders, through hatches, out into the eerie blackness. Covers came off the guns. Ammunition was ready. Over the battle phones came the brief announcement, "Two enemy surface craft reported."

Cruiser guns could obliterate the patrol vessels, but Halsey hoped to push further westward before discovery. The carriers were still not close enough for the launch. The enemy veered off without observing the task force. At 0415 hours, undetected, the *Hornet, Enterprise,* and the cruisers resumed base course 270°.

It dawned murky grey. The weather was foul, stormy. The task force pitched and rolled. Planes zipped off the flight deck of the *Enterprise* on morning patrol. Forty-two miles away, Lieutenant Wiseman, naval aviator, spied a Japanese patrol craft, the size and shape of a tugboat. Wiseman did not attack, complying with orders, and attempted unsuccessfully to avoid detection. Plummeting over the carrier, he dropped a message, reporting contact, stating he had been seen.

On board a Japanese patrol ship of the Northern Force, the lookout roused his skipper from a sound sleep to look at a plane high overhead. The captain, disinterested, rolled over in his bunk. The sailor again awakened him and reported, "Two of our beautiful carriers ahead, sir!"

The skipper stumbled out on deck and pondered them through his binoculars. "They're beautiful," he snapped, "But they're not ours."

He returned below and put a bullet through his head. Captainless, the vessel changed course and steamed off.

But other eyes watched Task Force 16. In the raging sea, the captain of the *Nitto Maru No. 23,* another patrol ship, expertly camouflaged, squinted through the wind and rain. He immediately called the radio operator.

From their lookout stations on the *Hornet,* bluejackets sighted this patrol vessel, distance 14,000 yards. To eliminate the possibility of the enemy sending a message, Halsey ordered the *Nashville* to sink her and quickly. No longer could the Americans evade a fight.

The *Nashville* opened up at 9000 yards, lobbing tons of steel toward the enemy picket. The entire area erupted. The sound roared back to the *Hornet* and *Enterprise* as the cruiser thundered at the target. The grey sky brightened with the hot flash of the guns. Black acrid smoke clouded the air. All along the *Nashville*'s deck, guns blazed red. But in the angry sea, accuracy was difficult. The *Nitto Maru No. 23* bobbed across the cruiser's bow. The captain ordered continuous fire, course converging on target. The salvos were fearsome. The *Nashville* checked fire momentarily as the enemy, wallowing in the trough of the sea, was totally obscured. Up popped the *Nitto Maru No. 23* again, unscathed. The Japanese radio operator got off the message: "Three enemy carriers sighted. Position, 600 miles east of Inubo Saki."

From the air, naval aviator J. Q. Roberts sighted the craft. He peeled off, his .50-caliber guns stuttering, scattering the sailors on her deck. His 500-lb. bomb missed by 100 feet.

In the *Hornet*'s ready room, Lieutenant John Sutherland, USN, deafened by the racket, raced out on deck. "I remember," he said, "thinking that it was a very curious way to watch my first active engagement. We stood on the flight deck watching the fire between our ship and the meager return from the Japs, much in the manner of a crowd watching a tennis match with their heads going back and forth. Well, if combat's like this, this will be fine."

The *Nashville*'s guns pumped away. The adversary refused to sink. With difficulty, Lieutenant W. Kirten, Jr., the gunnery officer, kept his temper. It was inconceivable that a cruiser could not demolish a tug.

Gaping in astonishment, Halsey angrily ordered the *Nashville* to close to point-blank range. But in the surging sea the *Nitto Maru No. 23* continued to drop from sight. It was painfully apparent that the *Nashville*'s shells were hitting the wave tops. The cruiser, checking her fire, swung to port, her turrets bearing on the starboard. Her guns flashed again. After the third salvo, the *Nitto Maru No. 23* finally went under, after evading 924 shells. The engagement had lasted 29 minutes.

Radio intelligence on the *Enterprise* indicated that the picket ship had already broadcast the position and the number of ships in the task force. Japanese radio traffic built up. American intelligence officers translated the plain language messages. There was no mistake. News of the carriers' approach had been received in Tokyo.

Halsey was dangerously exposed. His carriers were within range of shore-based bombers and open to attack by surface units. The problem, Halsey reasoned, was to weigh and accurately balance the proportionate risks to naval and air elements. Tactics were dominated by two controlling ideas: the enemy should not be given a chance to hit the carriers; the bombers must have enough fuel after the raid to give them a fighting chance of reaching China. Contact with the Japanese picket already had compromised secrecy. The prime consideration was to get the Army planes airborne before the arrival of shore-based bombers.

At the sound of the *Nashville*'s fire, Doolittle had raced to the *Hornet*'s bridge. Both he and Mitscher stood grim-faced. The colonel did some swift mental arithmetic. The task force was 668 miles from the heart of Tokyo, in latitude 35° 45′ N., longitude 153° 40′ W. If the ships maintained their present course and speed another nine hours, the hazards of the raid would not be exceptional. If they took off immediately, no one could predict the outcome.

In the wardroom, stewards' mates brought in heaping plates of bacon and scrambled powdered eggs, water oozing around them. And pancakes and fresh strawberries and toast and coffee. On the flight deck, other airmen, forgetting breakfast, manhandled baggage into the planes. The combat crews were sure, now, that it would be a daylight raid. They calculated on a 20% to 50% casualty minimum by enemy gunfire. As the carriers were 668 miles from the target, they understood there was little, if any, possibility of landing in China. It was almost certain they would ditch in a Japanese-dominated sea.

At 0800 hours, blinker lights flashed from the *Enterprise*. "Launch planes. To Col. Doolittle and his gallant command good luck and God bless you."

The colonel hastened down from the *Hornet*'s bridge and, in the ready room, calmly addressed his anxious crews. He ran through the schedule for the last time—run to Tokyo, bomb, fly south around the southern tip of Honshu Island, head for Chuchow, refuel. Avoid non-military targets, particularly the Palace. Take-off was beyond the line of safety. There were several hundred miles they didn't have gas for. If forced down, proceed to Chuchow and await orders.

The bull horns blasted, "Army personnel, man your planes." This was it. This was the point toward which they had been working. Few of them had ever been in combat; none of them knew what awaited. This was the hour that had been in their minds when they volunteered. This was the minute for which they had trained. Morale was high. [They were going to assault not just Tokyo, but a bitter memory, the memory of one humiliating day, 7 December 1941.]

Stand-by crews shouted, "You lucky devils! You lucky devils!" With fistfuls of money, they ran wildly about offering $150 to change places and make the run to Japan. Co-pilot Thadd Blanton would always remember that men were willing to pay $150 to die.

The weather continued rough, complicating the take-off. The chilling, frothing green water sloshed over the flight deck. Could they make it safely from a carrier rolling and pitching? On board the *Enterprise* and the escorts the loudspeakers blared, *"Hornet* preparing to launch bombers for the attack on Tokyo." Officers, cooks, engineers, seemingly everyone crowded decks, watched, waited.

Up and down the *Hornet's* flight deck, sixteen groups of charged-up airmen clustered by their planes. Lieutenant Jacob (call me "Shorty") Manch ran up to a plane, toting a fruit-cake tin, pleading with a bombardier to take along his collection of phonograph records. Manch already had the player in his own bomber. Lieutenant Harold F. "Doc" Watson frantically supervised the last minute change in spark plugs. Navigators fidgeted—locating Tokyo would be rough. They'd figured on a night run with star fixes. Now they would have to depend on the less-accurate sun lines. Crawling into the rear compartment of his plane, an enlisted man shouted to Corporal DeShazer, "We just got one chance in a thousand of making it." Machinist's Mate George Radulovich prayed.

Crews checked the planes from nose to tail, rechecked them, stowed their equipment, hoisted on board extra five-gallon cans of gasoline, listened for the pilots to tell them to start the engines.

Captain Davey Jones was fuming. The night before, when personnel had started fueling his plane, they had discovered a leak in the bomb-bay tank. Airdales patched it up, but the tank had been left empty all night to dry out. Just as the order came to man the planes, Jones' engineer along with machinists' mates finished filling up the crawlway tank, then climbed up to top off the wing tanks. Jones entered the plane to check the gas gauges. The left rear tank registered 30 gallons short. He called the engineer to crawl back on the left wing to service the tank. But someone had turned off the hose. There was no time.

Doolittle walked to his plane. Lieutenant Dick Cole was in the co-pilot's seat, starting through the checking routine. He did it hurriedly, knowing there was no need for haste, but unable to take it easy. Then the colonel eased himself into his seat. In other planes, other pilots and co-pilots went through the preflight routine.

Major Jack Hilger was informing his crew they wouldn't have enough gas to reach China. "The way things are now," he rasped, "we have about enough to get us within 200 miles of the China coast, and that's all. If anyone wants to withdraw, he can do it now. We can replace him from the men who are going to be left aboard. Nothing will ever be said about it, and it won't be held against you. It's your right. It's up to you." No one stirred.

Somewhere up the flight deck, in the line of silent, hulking planes, an engine coughed. Another plane started up, then another. Propellers lazily windmilled. Exhausts puffed as the engines caught with a roar.

The eyes of the task force focused on Doolittle. The big bomber needed all the runway it could get. With fifteen planes packed solidly behind, the colonel had only half the length of the deck ahead. It looked pitifully short. The men glanced from the aircraft to the mountainous seas. If the colonel's plane missed, the onrushing *Hornet* would slice it in two.

The carrier turned into the wind at 22 knots, course 310°. Chief Engineer Pat Creehan, Commander, USN, pushed the engines and his men to the breaking point to get the last fraction of speed needed to give the planes a head wind.

A Navy flight officer stood at the bow of the pitching ship, to the port, with a checkered flag in his hand. When the flag started swinging rapidly, Doolittle and Cole gave the engines more throttle. The colonel called through his intercom to crew chief Paul Leonard, crouched in the rear of the plane. "Everything all right, Paul?"

"Everything okay, Colonel."

The signal officer on the bow gauged the waves to put Doolittle's plane at the end of the runway just as the *Hornet* surged up to the crest. The colonel pushed his engines to full throttle. The roar shook the deck. Chocks were pulled from the wheels. Doolittle got the flag. Brakes were released. Airdales threw themselves prone on the deck so the wings would pass over them. With full flaps, engines at full throttle, the plane rumbled down the deck, slowly, then faster and faster. "He'll never make it," hollered a naval aviator. Waves reached for the wheels. Zoom! As the *Hornet*'s bow crashed down, Doolittle was airborne. He climbed, leveled off, circled.

Amid resounding cheers and whistles, Lieutenant Travis Hoover's plane raced down the flight deck. It faltered as it lifted up, fluttered, sank to within a few feet of the water. Suddenly, it soared upward, moving like a kangaroo over the horizon.

Planes 3, 4, 5, 6 escaped into the air. The sky was a canopy of B-25s. Sailors stared proudly at the American insignia painted on their wings and fuselages.

Ted Lawson in plane 7 forgot to put the flaps down, and narrowly escaped plummeting into the sea. Ski York in plane 8 yelled to his co-pilot, Lieutenant Bob Emmens, "Make damned sure those throttles don't slip back!" He watched the Navy signalman. The bomber vibrated with both throttles wide open. Flaps were down, controls all the way back in their laps. The flagman dropped his arms.

York released the brakes, and they began to roll, left wheel on the white line down the deck. The superstructure shot from sight as the plane passed it by a bare eight feet away from the right wing tip. The B-25 jumped into the air and leveled out. York started taking off flaps, throttles back to save the gas. They adjusted their power settings, checked the compass, and set course for Tokyo. Emmens thought about the piles of razor blades, candy, and cartons of cigarettes he had purchased on board, amused at himself for buying so much as if he would be gone a year.

Planes 9, 10, 11, 12, 13 were soon airborne. There was little formation. Aircraft taking off early dared not hover over the *Hornet* as they'd burn too much fuel. Each circled to the right, flew over the carrier, and lined the axis of the ship up with the drift sight. The course of the *Hornet* was emblazoned in huge figures from the gun turret abaft the island to enable the raiders to swing off on the proper heading for Tokyo.

Don Smith started his engines and watched Major Hilger, his element leader, clear the deck. The signal officer motioned Smith to ease forward. The plane failed to budge. Smith checked again to make sure the brakes were off. Looking out, he noticed the airdales hadn't removed the blocks from the wheels. Once these were yanked out, it took Smith three more minutes to taxi from the parking position to the take-off line. With the *Hornet* pitching, the bomber could only advance as the bow splashed down.

At the take-off position, Smith and co-pilot Griff Williams locked the brakes, checked the flaps, which were full. They were given the signal to increase throttle. They got the signal to go. The plane sped down the deck. The bow dropped away suddenly, leaving the bomber in the air, doing 90 mph. The wheels came up. Williams started easing back on the throttle and propeller control. The flaps were milked. Air speed was 150 mph, so Smith throttled back to long-range cruise. He wanted to catch up with Hilger, fast disappearing in the haze.

The last plane, Bill Farrow's, seemed jinxed from the start. The instant it was ready to taxi to the take-off line, the carrier lurched sharply. The bomber slid backwards. For a split second it looked as if the B-25 would plunge into the sea. Seamen rushed toward the skidding aircraft, lashing lines to its nose. The lines snapped. Every man who could, took a hand hold and hung onto the front end of the plane. By sheer human strength the bomber held the deck. Tragically, Machinist Mate Robert W. Wall backed into the whirling props and lost his arm.

Once in take-off position, Jake DeShazer took station in the nose. He was horrified at the sight. The plastic nose, instead of being wind-tight and rounded, was damaged. DeShazer confronted a jagged hole, more than a foot in diameter. Already, Farrow was speeding up the engines. The flagman was about to give the signal. Delay was impossible. It was a perfect take-off.

As Farrow's plane surged forward, the previously-scheduled air-raid drill began in Tokyo. Officials placed the city under "first alarm" discipline. No sirens screeched. The population didn't seek shelter or participate. The man in the street went about his business, manifesting only casual curiosity. Tokyo fire-fighting companies demonstrated as air-raid wardens stood by. Japanese air maneuvers over the city were frequent; pursuits engaged in mock dog fights; army enlisted men hoisted and lowered barrage balloons along the waterfront. At the British Embassy two squads of firemen turned to for a brief time. Designated personnel at the American Embassy went through the motions required by regulation. By 1100 hours the American air-raid warden was teeing off on the golf course.

The General Staff of the Japanese Navy had received the message from the *Nitto Maru No. 23*. This was the first contact with the enemy task force since 10 April, when radio intelligence had informed them of its location. Upon receipt of the message, the General Staff estimated that the raid would come on the morning of the 19th. By their computations, the carriers would be forced, because of the operating radius of their fighter planes, to close to within 200 miles of the coast before launching.

The 26th Air Flotilla commander, upon notification, alerted his reconnaissance and attack units. At 1145 hours, 24 carrier-type fighters, equipped with extra fuel tanks, and 29 medium bombers roared off from Kisarazu Air Base. The patrol sighted two planes, position 580 miles bearing 85° from the air station. Japanese pilots erred by identifying them as "the flying boat type." No alarm was given.

Skimming over the wave tops, racing for the Japanese coast, Doolittle's and Hoover's crews spotted the two enemy planes far in the distance. This was the worst part of the raid—this time when the carriers were far behind and the target was still ahead. Now was the time to listen to Tokyo radio. The pilots kept watch on the instrument panels. Navigators looked at their maps which showed Tokyo's precise position and rechecked their dead reckoning. They glanced at the compass needle, wondered if it were correct, and dreaded the moment when they would know whether their figures were incredibly right or fatally wrong. They scanned the waste of sky and water. Excited and tense, crews routinely checked out their equipment, tested their guns by firing a few bursts, poured gasoline from the cans into the turret tank; then, chopping holes in them, heaved them out of the plane. A rough calculation indicated that each plane had consumed eight five-gallon cans during the warmup on the *Hornet*. Forty precious gallons had vanished before they'd set a course for Tokyo. Two thousand, two hundred miles of flying lay ahead.

While airmen were transferring the gas, the sun came out. They had flown beyond the overcast and broken out into uncovered day. Two hundred miles from the target, there was nothing above them but pure, dry sky. From now on the raiders began sighting fishing vessels, hundreds of them. Not a pilot doubted that he had been reported, that interception was imminent.

In plane 4, Corporal Bert Jordan pressed the trigger of his .50 calibers. Nothing happened. The guns had gone haywire. Desperately, he fumbled about to find the trouble. He called to the pilot over the intercom. Lieutenant Everett "Brick" Holstrom couldn't understand him. The crawlway tank blocked the way forward. Nearing the coast, Jordan discovered the electrical lead to the turret was not connected. It had been removed on the *Hornet* and not hooked up again.

Ski York's navigator, Nolan Herndon, gave a corrected flight heading to compensate for the strong wind from the right front quarter. York checked and refigured the power and propeller settings against the air speed. The engines droned on endlessly.

Emmens, the co-pilot, worried about an engine going blooey over the ocean and the possibility of encountering

Japanese Zeros. Dave Pohl, the gunner, dumped the last tin of gasoline into the auxiliary tank.

Emmens took the controls while York computed the fuel consumption. His arithmetic showed the plane gulping gas at an incredible rate. Instead of the normal 72 or 75, he was burning 98 gallons per hour. Perhaps the gauge was fouled up. Perhaps they had a leak. Perhaps it was that damn mechanic back in Sacramento who had adjusted the carburetor.

Landfall was imminent. Herndon again unfolded his charts of the territory ahead. He moved into the pilot's compartment and inspected the reading on the bomb-bay tank. Cripes! were they burning fuel!

The crew faced a critical decision. They sorted and resorted the possibilities. They could crash land in Japan—this was out of the question. They could fly their originally-planned course south, around the lower end of Japan, then west, ditching in the China Sea. They could strike out for Soviet territory. The Russians might even refuel them for the trip to Free China. After all, they were allies against the Germans. "I guess you guys remember Doolittle didn't exactly issue a direct order not to go to Russia, but he made it plenty obvious it wasn't a good idea," said York.

In Doc Watson's plane, 9, the bombardier, Sergeant Wayne Bissell, sat on the right in the ship's nose. Light filtering through the conical windshield gave his face a bilious tinge as he brushed his hand lightly across the .30 caliber. Along the near wall were the cold air ventilator, the camera gun stowage bracket, and gun mount socket. On Bissell's left were his bomb controls and instrument panel. Behind him the plane was divided. Topside was the pilot's compartment. The lower level was a tunnel about four feet high which led to the navigator's well and front entrance hatch.

Watson and his co-pilot, Jim Parker, faced a windshield. They sat amid a maze of instruments—dozens of dials and switches, knobs and indicators, lights and buttons, gauges and gismos, whose function controlled the plane. The main instrument panel was before them. The instrument rheostats, power-plant controls, and emergency hydraulic selector valve were centered between them.

Behind the pilots, Lieutenant Tom Griffin was plotting the course. He studied the driftmeter and compass, made his calculations, took the sun sights. Still farther back behind the navigator, separated by the crawlway and the bomb bay, was Sergeant Eldred V. Scott, firing a few bursts, testing the .50 calibers and turret. To his rear was the after escape hatch.

Element leader Jack Hilger had lost Bill Farrow's plane in the clouds. Plane 16 was falling steadily behind the pack—far behind. The wind whistled through the gaping hole in the bomber's nose. Jake DeShazer and co-pilot Bobby Hite tried stuffing it with an overcoat, which the wind swept away. There was no panic. But they realized that with the damaged nose, the streamline effect of their B-25 was greatly reduced; their gas consumption was well above normal.

It was nearly noon.

The planes were streaking for Inubo Saki. Tokyo lies 63 miles due west of this mark, its housing spread around the northern and western shores of the bay. To the south, along the west shore is Yokohama. The city of Nagoya is off the southern coast of Japan along Ise Bay,

125 miles west of the capital. A hundred miles beyond are the cities of Osaka and Kobe, whose suburbs join around the north shore of Osaka Bay with no open country between.

These were the targets. A line drawn from the Boso Peninsula to Chuchow would touch nearly all four cities. The assignments of the 16 bombers were well equalized. Each would fly about the same distance. To locate the targets expeditiously, the B-25s would have to check their orientation marks somewhere along the Boso Peninsula. The common problem was to fly into the Tokyo Bay region and then make further reckonings.

Doolittle saw the Japanese coast. To his disbelief and annoyance, he discovered the plane was 50 miles north of Tokyo. They would have to fly extra, needless miles. Looking out to the left, Doolittle and Cole saw another B-25 dip its wings. Trav Hoover was on schedule.

Pounding in toward the coast, other planes badly misjudged their positions and made landfall to the north and to the south. Only two of the 16—Doc Watson and Lieutenant Dick Joyce—soared in on the exact course. Thus more by accident than by design, the raid assumed an aspect which mystified the enemy. The attack fell on Tokyo from the north, the east, and the south—an unplanned deception, misleading the Japanese as to the base of operation.

The colonel took advantage of the navigational error and approached Tokyo from a northerly direction with Trav Hoover close behind.

They hurtled along at tree-top level. Suddenly, the colonel spotted Japanese fighters, dead ahead, 1000 feet above. He sheered off to the left. The enemy veered right. Doolittle straightened out and flew toward the city. The pursuits followed. Quickly, the colonel turned sharply, racing into a valley formed by two hills, the olive-drab camouflage of the bombers blending into the Japanese countryside, deceiving the fighters. Once through the valley, the B-25s turned right and resumed course.

The suburbs of Tokyo came into view; then the whole city materialized—the Palace, houses, factories, warehouses, highways. The populace displayed no signs of alarm. At a small military camp on the outskirts, soldiers stood at attention with a sworded officer beside them. They looked exactly like all the photographs of all the Japanese soldiers the Americans had ever seen. Training planes carried on their work of landing and taking off. Tramcars were running. Airfields were unalerted. The Japanese were busy working and playing. Tokyo lay naked under the bombsights of the B-25s.

A country school principal saw two planes with American insignia pass low over his building. Fearfully, he glanced at his district's air raid protection, holes dug in the ground, and at the weapons, bamboo spears to beat off enemy paratroopers.

At the Sumida River, which snakes through northern Tokyo, Hoover turned westward toward his objective, and Doolittle proceeded on a southwest line straight across the city.

The colonel's bombardier, Fred Braemer, checking the gradations on the two-bit bombsight, scrutinized the city as the B-25 came in. He was all set. He had fused the bombs; mounted and armed the .30-caliber machine gun. Now he searched for the target amid factories and warehouses. He located the check points that intelligence had mentioned in the jumble below.

Doolittle gunned his engines and lifted to 1500 feet,

the bomb-run altitude. "Approaching target," the colonel shouted into the intercom. The bomb-bay doors clanked open at 1210 hours Tokyo time. On the instrument panel the red light blinked, indicating the first 500-lb. incendiary cluster had dropped. The red light pulsated three more times in quick succession. The bombs fell right down into the center of Tokyo—convincingly.

Relieved of 2000 lbs., the B-25 leaped in the air. Doolittle jammed the controls forward, the plane dropping to housetop level for withdrawal.

Antiaircraft guns sprang to life. There was a bevy of black bursts. More guns jumped into action from a dozen points. The black puffs drifted up, a flurry of them, all around. Doolittle's plane quivered from a near miss.

The Japanese .20 millimeters were thump, thump, thumping away. An eager-beaver private kept pecking away with a machine gun. The tracers spat from a corner of an airfield. "My fingers itched for action when I saw the enemy plane," recalled the Japanese private.

Doolittle jacked up the rpms on both engines. Ahead the colonel spotted an aircraft factory with spanking new training planes, red and silver, standing on the apron. He resisted the impulse to strafe with machine gun fire. Escape was essential.

At the offices of the *Japan Times,* Dr. Iwao Kawai, chief editorial writer, peered from the window at crowds below gaping skyward. He saw antiaircraft guns firing, but he thought it was part of the alert. It seemed strange to practice with live shells.

P. E. Sato had taken the streetcar to go shopping in downtown Tokyo. He was casually walking across a bridge, when he heard the ear-splitting roar of engines overhead and saw a "very beautiful" plane flashing past, low. Nobody on that bridge noticed the American insignia. They knew nothing about the incendiary bombs dropping on other parts of the city. After the aircraft disappeared, Sato continued his shopping. "That afternoon," he remembered, "nothing had changed. People were living in the usual manner."

Business flowed as usual. Buses, trolleys, and motor vehicles moved without interruption. No siren sounded. Lunch crowds leisurely finished their meals and returned to their offices. Theaters opened for matinee performances.

At Uyeno Fine Arts Museum, Admiral Shigetaro Shimada, Navy Minister, continued his tour, unperturbed, inspecting the Japanese sword collection. He couldn't resist holding a fancy dagger in his hand and, to his aide, whispered, "Beautiful, isn't it."

Mr. Oiwa, editor of the *Silk Digest,* was in the streets of downtown Tokyo. He saw a plane overhead and wondered where it had come from. Standing nearby, a friend warned that it was an American bomber, not Japanese. They walked down the street together, arguing, speculating over the plane's home base.

"It came from Hawaii," screamed Mrs. Iwata as she ushered her guest out of the house and homeward. "More will follow." At that moment, Mrs. Iwata decided to have her husband, a plumbing works executive, dig an air-raid shelter in their back yard. The radio was still playing "The Blue Danube Waltz."

Swooping in low, pouring on the coal, Hoover rocketed along the Sumida River so fast that he was instantly upon the target. Split seconds remained to pull up. He leveled at 900 feet. "There's our target," Hoover said, crisply, authoritatively. Dick Miller, the bombardier, saw it too. He took dead aim at the center of a gigantic factory and released the bombs. "Bombs away—let's get out of here!" hollered Miller. Concussions jolted the plane.

The buildings below winked at them in flashes. White flashes, red flashes. Then an enormous pillar of smoke and flame tumbled upward. "We got two direct hits!" Lieutenant Fitzhugh, the co-pilot, yelped. Instead of hitting their primary objective, a powder works, they'd smashed an adjacent factory and warehouse in a heavily-congested industrial area.

Watching for pursuits, Sergeant Radney whirled the turret. It stuck fast on the left wing stop. Arduously, he swung the guns toward the rear, but the azimuth electrical motor had burned out. The flak, white cottony wisps, floated upward. Far to the left in Doolittle's sector, Hoover noted ack-ack bursts making a track across the sky.

The American offensive stalled. In the 30 minutes which followed Hoover's departure from the *Hornet,* eight more bombers had launched, but their advance toward Japan was delayed through faulty navigation and mechanical failures. During this hiatus, the city sounded the alarm, and its military and air defenses were committed to action.

In plane 3, Lieutenant Bob Gray missed the direct approach to Tokyo. Striking the mainland 15 miles south of Tokyo, Gray wheeled westward across the Boso Peninsula and whistled into the city from the southeast. Batteries protecting the waterfront threw up flak. Bursts scattered in all directions, tracking the bomber as it bore toward the objective. Slamming in at housetop level,

Gray jumped to 1500 feet to unload his bombs onto a steel works, chemical factory, and gas plant. Black rolls of smoke spread majestically and rolled skyward. The ack-ack thickened. Pushing the bomber's nose down, shoving the throttles forward, Gray dove back to the earth and retraced his course toward the bay.

The ship thundered as Aden Jones, the bombardier, blazed away with his .30 caliber, stitching the streets below. As the plane shot over a factory yard, Jones pulled the trigger and felt the gun pound. Bullets whined into the dirt. There was wild confusion as men ducked for cover. Navigator Charlie Ozuk noticed 15 or 20 men slump as if hit by the bombardier's fire. Gray droned off across Tokyo Bay. Twelve enemy pursuits passed overhead, but continued on their way.

Plane 4, its turret and .50 calibers inoperative, sped across the ocean at a 75-foot altitude, course 270°. Bert Jordan was still trying to communicate with Holstrom over the intercom. Once the crew emptied the last crawlway tank, Jordan scrambled forward with the news the turret was out of commission, the .50 calibers unserviceable, the left wing tank leaking slowly.

A 15° compass error had buggered up their navigation. Holstrom made landfall 90 miles south of the target area, adding 180 miles to their journey. Quickly, pilot and co-pilot checked their dials. They barked out reminders to the crew. At the rate the engines were wolfing down the fuel, they were already considerably short of gas. Holstrom wheeled northward toward the objective and immediately moved against the traffic of outbound Americans, who were trailed by enemy fighters.

Sub-Lieutenant Umekawa was flying over an airfield when he spotted the bomber running in at low altitude.

Together with another pursuit, Umekawa attacked the invader.

Co-pilot Lucien Youngblood was still transferring the last bit of gas from the bomb bay tank when Holstrom spied two pursuits roaring in fast. The B-25 darted beneath them. Umekawa sprayed the Americans with tracers, firing continually on the approach. The bullets whizzed past the pilot's compartment. In the blood-pounding excitement the crew cursed helplessly—the damned .50 calibers were useless. There was no protection.

Two more fighters cut across the bow at 1500 feet, ready to peel off. This sort of attack had the effect of a concentrated barrage. Holstrom, changing throttle settings, picked up the speed to 250 mph. He yelled to Bob Stephens, the bombardier, to let go with his .30 caliber and jettison the bombs so the plane could outrun the enemy. Stephens placed the arming handle in safe position and salvoed the bombs into the sea, 75 feet above the water. The B-25 leaped, shot forward, turning south away from Tokyo and the target.

Sub-Lieutenant Umekawa gave chase and opened fire at short range. The bomber was too fast, its evasive tactics too perfect. Noticing the gauge, Umekawa realized he was short of gas. He veered and sped back to his base.

Davey Jones in plane 5 was trailed into the mainland by Lieutenant Dean Hallmark's ship. As they neared the coast, they dropped to water level and crossed the beach at 50 feet. Flying ten minutes overland, Jones failed to orient himself. Was he too far north? He turned south. He wished to hell he knew where Tokyo was. Time was escaping.

His take-off that morning had been attended with

extraordinary stress—the bombs had been loaded and the plane fueled while the first B-25s had taken off down the runway. The tanks hadn't been topped off. The crew had worried through the past two hours over the gas shortage, which was increasing as they floundered, hunting their target.

Jones determined to loose his eggs on the first suitable objective and withdraw. Suddenly, the plane was in the mouth of Tokyo Bay. Jones swerved toward the city. Hallmark's plane followed for a short distance before they lost visual contact.

A multitude of targets flashed by as Jones crossed the bay. He decided to strike southwestern Tokyo instead of turning east and flying around the city to his pre-assigned sector.

Heavy flak was everywhere. Jones' plane had been mousetrapped. There was nothing they could do until they dropped the bombs. They could hear the hollow *boom-boom-boom-boom* of the flak pounding just behind them in overlapping measures of four—the sharp, piercing *crack!* of a single shell exploding close by.

Off the waterfront, Jones picked an oil tank and a power plant as targets one and two. The first two missiles struck the tank and demolished the plant. The building collapsed convulsively into a churning wave of coal black smoke, which rolled turbulently in all directions.

With a grinding howl of engines, the B-25 flipped over on one wing and swung screaming around to the left. Instantly, Jones sighted a large factory. He watched bombs from the incendiary cluster pitch into its roof.

Lightened, the B-25 lurched upward violently. The bomb-bay doors closed. Jones dove to tree-top level. The wind strummed against the cylindrical panes of the bombardier's windows as the plane plunged lower. Denver

Truelove noticed bursts shooting up from the hills, myriads of them, chasing the plane as it whipped over roofs. The flak men, trying to hit the low-level bomber, fired into the city opposite, raking dwellings and shops.

Hallmark in plane 6 turned for northern Tokyo and its designated target, the steel mills. The bomber swept in through a crisscrossing barrage of fire that hammered up from the ground. Three bombs dropped. To escape the ack-ack pitching toward them, Hallmark turned sharply, circled, and began a second run on the target. Navigator Chase Nielsen saw three bombs "blow all hell" out of the southern end of the steel mill.

Hallmark's assault was the last upon interior Tokyo. Jones' run on the harbor front coincided with the shifting of operations to that region. Now the distribution of attack around the bay shore had such seeming method the Japanese concluded that the main objective of the raid was the industrial and shipping installations along the waterfront.

All but one B-25 which bombed the bay region came in from the southwest. In striking this sector, the Americans moved against the strongest line of Tokyo's defenses. Balloons blanketed vital installations to the north and west, supported by antiaircraft guns ringing the shoreline.

Ted Lawson made landfall near Kasumiga Lake. The crew of plane 7 noticed the people on the white sand beach gazing up, waving, and little boys throwing stones at the low-flying aircraft. Co-pilot Dean Davenport glimpsed a playground with a tall flagpole and a Rising Sun spanking in the breeze. Halfway between the coast and Tokyo, while Lawson wove through the mountain passes, Dave Thatcher, the gunner, observed the skidding shapes of pursuits, like profiles from identification cards, flying high above, going in the opposite direction.

Over the interphone Lawson instructed Thatcher to test the turret. It failed to revolve. The 24-volt generator was snafued. Even with the emergency battery snapped on, it refused to budge. Trained toward the rear, the .50 calibers would be handicapped in a fight with Nipponese interceptors. Lawson raised the ship's nose, the tail slanting down. Thatcher triggered a few bursts. The intercom sets were still. Each airman realized the plane had little defense. They worried about the gas consumption. The auxiliary tanks were empty. Thatcher tried the turret again. It rotated perfectly—the plane had built up enough emergency juice.

The bomber ripped south over the Boso Peninsula to a point opposite the Tokyo waterfront. Crossing the bay, the crew spotted an aircraft carrier at anchor. Over the intercom they pleaded, "Let's drop an egg on it!" But Lawson passed it up.

The B-25 made a straight east-west run across the target. Lawson skirted the corner of the bay, gave the engines full throttle, zoomed to 1400 feet as Davenport adjusted the prop pitch. Buildings loomed larger.

The low approach at high speed limited observation. Barreling in at minimum level, pilots had difficulty reconciling the scene with their data for target finding. They had to stay low and could see only a short distance ahead. If they climbed for a quick look, they drew AA fire.

Lawson was not running along the designated line of objectives. He dumped three 500-lb. demolitions into a factory district and, according to bombardier Bob Clever's report, dropped the incendiary beyond the third target in a densely settled residential area.

Every gun of the Japanese seemed to open up on Lawson. There was one sequence of bursts, coming at regular intervals, directly in front, directly on course, each one closer than the last, until one exploded right in front of the plane. The crew partly heard, partly felt its dull thud. There was another thud behind them. Lawson went into a screeching power dive and left the zone with the air speed indicator registering over 350 mph. Off to the right, beyond the Imperial Palace, they saw the fires started by Doolittle, smoldering dismally like a city dump.

Frantic about gas consumption, Ski York's crew in plane 8 continued to contemplate landing at Vladivostok. Sergeant Laban, atop the bomb-bay tank, was reading the gauge when they sighted the Japanese coast. In the navigator's seat, Herndon reported the course from Tokyo to Vladivostok was 300°. Swiftly refiguring fuel consumption, Captain York decided his plane would fall at least 300 miles short of China.

York and Emmens saw what appeared to be a hulking aircraft carrier, paralleling the coast directly ahead. The plane sheered sharply, changing course to avoid her. Staying out of range, the B-25 headed for shore. In a matter of minutes they were racing over dry land, hunting for Tokyo. Rice paddies and farm lands flashed by beneath. An old man, tending his cow, pushed back his broad-brimmed hat to look up more comfortably as he waved his staff at the hedge-hopping plane.

Dave Pohl rotated the turret slowly. Far to the right, he spotted nine Japanese fighters winging in the opposite direction. The B-25 was suddenly over Tokyo. York pulled up to 1500 feet and attacked the first likely target —a factory installation with four stacks.

"Open your bomb-bay doors, Herndon," York shouted

and, to Emmens, "Jesus, that would be a fine thing at a time like this—to forget to open your bomb-bay doors!"

The target disappeared. "Bombs away!" hollered Herndon. Then, after a pause, "Bomb-bay doors closed." Rocking jolts signaled the bombs had exploded. With air speed jumping higher, the plane dove and took evasive action.

The ship's shudder indicated to York that the .30 caliber was pounding away. Herndon had his sights on a row of training planes lined up on a flying field. A smell reminiscent of the Fourth of July drifted backward into the cockpit. Turning northwest, the B-25 approached the foothills on a heading for Russia.

B-25s 9 and 10, piloted by Watson and Joyce, were bombing the eastern shore. These two had come into Tokyo by the shortest route, their navigators right on course, and, in so doing, closed the interval between themselves and the element ahead. The first planes over had caught the enemy fighters on the ground, something no pilot thought would happen. But now, from every fighter base around Tokyo, interceptors took off full throttle in pursuit. Watson and Joyce were the conspicuous targets.

Watson bore straight into the coast, zigzagged between mountains, scraping the rice paddies so closely, he startled wide-eyed farmers and drilling soldiers.

Rocketing in just above the ground, Watson saw Tokyo come up suddenly, the whole jigsaw of the city sprawling before him. The crew stared down. Watson talked on the intercom, giving orders, and was amazed and pleased, too, at the calm sound of the men's voices.

With apparent disregard for heavy AA fire, Watson sped from the city's northeast corner diagonally to the southwest toward the target. This forced him over the batteries concentrated around the Imperial Palace and those covering the waterfront. He swept in through the crisscrossing barrage of fire that hammered up from the ground.

Come on up you Japanese fighters, fire Japanese anti-aircraft, come on you bastards, knock hell out of us if you can, for we sure are going to bomb hell out of you. Now straight over the rooftops, straight into the heart of the Imperial City of Tokyo. Don't touch the Palace, but I'm going back one day and smack the Mikado right on his dome. Come on, hit us, bring us down if you can—if we are going to die, O.K., but if this crate falls, I'm going to put it nose down, full throttle, and bend it around a street. I'll take plenty of you bastards with me when I hit.

The bomb-bay doors opened. The crew heard the laboring roar of the engines. The signal from the bombardier came. Watson's eyes darted from his direction indicator, to his air speed, to his altimeter, then back to his indicator. He waited for the bomb release light to blink. *Blink. Blink. Blink. Blink.* The crew felt each bomb as it snapped out of the shackles. The Tokyo Gas and Electric Engineering Company was the target, but Watson was too busy evading ack-ack to observe the damage. Scott, the gunner, kept looking out at the wings, expecting to see holes in the skin any minute. Watching on the right, Jim Parker, the co-pilot, glimpsed one bomb smacking the northernmost building. Two demolitions and one incendiary crashed into the target; the last demolition, four seconds late, landed 500 yards beyond in a congested housing district. Scotty looked back. What he saw was four streams of tracers shooting up past the plane. He stared down. A pursuit was rushing up at their belly, firing at close range. The .50 calibers chattered. Bullets whipped from the muzzles, every fifth missile glowing bright cherry red. The interceptor winged off.

Watson racked the plane into a turn, slammed up the throttles, and flattened out over the rows of buildings. A voluminous barrage of bursting shells dogged him all the way as he flew south over Yokohama, past the Yokosuka Naval Station, toward the sea. Tense muscles relaxed. It was done. They had bombed Tokyo.

Lieutenant Dick Joyce in plane 10 turned westward toward upper Tokyo Bay. The clouds fell away, and he saw an aircraft carrier steaming defiantly. Her .20 millimeters flared, but the fire was ineffective. Joyce made a long, straight run on his target. Two demolition bombs on the Japan Special Steel Company were direct hits. Fleetingly, Lieutenant Crouch, the navigator, saw the walls of two buildings "scrambling men between them." The third and the incendiary were unloaded in a heavy industrial and residential section, about a quarter of a mile from their primary objective.

By the time the bomb-bay doors banged shut, Joyce was caught in an antiaircraft bracket with puffs and bursts coming close and catching up fast. One shell tore into the fuselage just ahead of the automatic stabilizer.

Americans confined in a school in the Denenshofu district saw Joyce flying west along the Tamagawa River, ack-ack wrapped so close around him they watched for the bomber to fall in flames.

Safety was far away. On both sides, Japanese fighters boxed Joyce in. Everywhere he turned, his eyes saw something happening. Two pursuits peeled off and came down together, firing, tracers ripping into the bomber's left wing. Joyce shot beneath them. His turret gunner cut loose with a deafening burst. Shell casings clattered on the flight deck. Another fighter bore down from high in front. Joyce's .50 calibers spoke again. His .30 caliber spat like a cat. The pursuits streaked in.

Gaining speed, Joyce dropped beneath them, his rate-of-climb needle pointing down, way down. To the left, three Nakajima 97s were in hot pursuit, but could not catch the fleeing bomber. Co-pilot Roy Stork pointed to a group of Zeros reaching for altitude, trailing the B-25, getting set. Joyce swung sharply to the west and sped toward the mountains. Gunner Eddie Horton whirled again and saw one fighter. He got in a burst at it coming, another broadside, and a burst going away. The tracers splattered it. The enemy was smoking.

Joyce escaped the area of sudden death and cleared the mainland of Japan ten miles west of Yokohama, encountering light and ineffective AA fire. Eluding another interceptor attack with a 2000-foot-per-minute climb, the plane, the last assigned to Tokyo proper, flew out of sight of land, and headed for Oshima Strait.

Thousands of Japanese were unaware that for the past hour Tokyo was under attack. Others were directly affected.

It was lunch time at Waseda Middle School. At the noon faculty meeting, members discussed plans for attending the funeral of a colleague. Outside on the playground, students whooped and romped through noonday exercises while others lunched in the dining hall. Suddenly, without warning, a bomber thundered in low. Kikujiro Suzuki thought the planes Japanese until he saw a classmate convulse and jump as an incendiary thudded into him. He lay quite still.

Opposite the school Mrs. Ryu Aoki had just bade good-bye to her husband and two sons, who were off to spend

Saturday with grandfather. She was staying home to tend her two younger daughters, aged seven and four, when, startled, she heard the racket above her. Running out of the house, she stared open-mouthed. A plane screamed over the tree tops, and black objects hurtled down into her roof.

Mr. Seikichi Honjo, her next-door neighbor, was sipping beer with a friend. As the noise increased, he stormed outside without taking time to put on his pants. Horrified, he saw two incendiaries land. Mrs. Aoki, clutching her two children, fled toward him. "Fire! Fire!" Honjo sprinted to the Aoki's, scaled the side of the house "like an acrobat," and saw the roof "just red all over." Quickly, with a shirt, he doused the fire. Even then Mrs. Aoki refused to believe it had been an air raid. Honjo, his eyebrows singed, was honored for bravery by the local police.

Mr. Katsuzo Yoshida, a hat maker by trade, was home that Saturday. When he heard the whine of aircraft engines, he stepped outside and watched incendiaries pitch into the Okasaki Hospital. In dismay, he saw orderlies and students carrying the sick from the burning building. Katsumi Kaneta, a graduate of Waseda University, saw the "big damage." "I thought," he said dejectedly, "that humanism cannot beat war, because the first bomb was dropped at a hospital. It was a cynical fact."

Mrs. Midori Dobashi was ready to go shopping when the air-raid warning sounded. Rushing upstairs, she discovered a black object gushing smoke in her four-mat room. Racing downstairs to the bathroom, she soaked a straw mat in water, returned upstairs, and calmly blanketed the fire. In another room she found the ceiling aflame. With a bamboo pole topped by soggy straw, she dabbed away and extinguished the blaze.

In another section of Tokyo, Minoru Iida heard the roar of a plane. Stepping outside his father's grocery store, he watched a bomber with American insignia raining black destruction. Minoru darted down the street screaming, "Enemy plane! Enemy plane! This is an air raid!" Suddenly, he saw a dark, foot-long object lying under the eaves of a house, hissing, smoking. Running back to the grocery, Minoru snatched the sand bucket, and sprinted back to smother the bomb. With pail in hand, Minoru proceeded down the street throwing sand on incendiaries as he found them.

At Tokyo Sophia University, the Reverend Bruno Bitter, S.J., thought the sirens part of the drill. When the bombs began detonating, citizens in his area scrambled and climbed on roofs or chimneys to get a better view. "It was a thrill rather than a frightening event," Father Bitter said.

John Morris, an American citizen, happened to be in the Ginza, Tokyo's main thoroughfare, headed for a doctor's appointment. When the warning sounded, no one paid attention, sure that the alarm was the regular mid-day signal.

The sirens cheered Otto D. Tolischus, *New York Times* correspondent, languishing in the Tokyo Detention Prison. Guards sprang down the corridors, double-locking the cell doors, gesticulating that this was no drill. Tolischus felt jubilant. During the first few nights of his incarceration, he had heard alarms and had rushed to the windows to listen, filled with hope. But each time Tolischus realized it was not an American attack, but fire engines.

From the window of a middle school building, Hiroichi Yamaguchi and his classmates whooped it up, excited by the sight of a low-flying bomber and the rapid fire of the antiaircraft guns. They were blinded momentarily by the reflection of the plane hurtling in just above their heads, dropping incendiaries. "The enemy has come from a field on Oshima Island," explained the teacher.

At the American Embassy, Ambassador Joseph C. Grew and his associates were just going to lunch when they heard the din outside. They went to the roof, where they gawked at a bomber shooting in low as if to crash, then leveling off at the tree tops. One, two, three, over they came. Residents of the Embassy thought the planes were Japanese. Off in the distance, they saw smoke spiraling skyward; to the left, a plane enveloped in black puffs. Had the gunners of the antiaircraft batteries lost their heads?

At the Argentine Embassy, Ramon Lavalle rushed to the roof and saw four bombers hedge-hopping not more than 100 feet off the ground. Looking down the streets, where the bombs detonated, he noticed Japanese running everywhere, pushing, shouting, screaming. The scrub woman at the Embassy tore upstairs, swinging her mop, and cried, "If these raids go on, we'll all go mad."

Stanislawa Tokalewska, a Polish resident of Tokyo, saw bombs career into the factory district, gutting one building completely. Hundreds of women scurried homeward to get buckets to help the local fire guards, trying vainly to smother the flames raging out of control. Antiaircraft gunners, almost berserk, started firing haphazardly into the sky.

Classes over, Eiji Inoue, books under his arm, walked toward home. He was startled by a low-flying plane with strange-sounding engines. Far to the right he saw barrages from antiaircraft guns line the sky. Down the street a huge black cloud of smoke erupted. "He dropped a bomb! He dropped a bomb! Let's go help!" shouted Eiji to his classmates. Collecting more students on the way, they raced toward the rapidly-burning movie house. Yellow and black smoke was pouring from the doors. Occasional flames pierced the smoke. Volunteer fire fighters tried to extinguish the blaze with a bucket brigade. Fire trucks careened up the street and stopped. Firemen battered the theater's walls and smashed windows in their efforts to douse the conflagration.

Plane 11, Ross Greening's, the first B-25 assigned to Yokohama, made landfall to the north and turned south toward the Boso Peninsula. Shortly after crossing Kasumiga Lake, four interceptors sprang out of nowhere. Hugging the ground, barreling beneath power lines, Greening successfully evaded their fire except for a few tracers which ripped into his right wing.

Sergeant Mel Gardner, the .50 calibers bucking in his hands, angrily whipped his guns forward. Bullets slammed into two pursuits. One fell away in flames.

The attack slowed. In the lull Greening sighted what resembled a thatched village but, upon close inspection, it proved to be an elaborately camouflaged tank farm. With fighters close on his heels, Greening forsook his primary target and bombed immediately. From an altitude of 600 feet—one, two, three, four—bombardier Bill Birch watched the terrific explosions. Huge sheets of flame burst upward. Greening and co-pilot Ken Reddy were jerked right out of their seats and, despite their harnesses, banged against the top of the cockpit. Greening kept thinking, "Oh, if my wife could see me now." The B-25 turned east to sea and outran the pursuits. To their rear, the Americans saw a gigantic column of black smoke.

An American teacher at Tsuda College, Miss Florence Wells, was on the Tokyo interurban train as it ground to a stop at the Yokohama Station. A guard sprinted down the platform, yelling, "Everybody out! Go down to the passage under the tracks!"

"Why?" shouted Miss Wells.

"It's orders!"

The travelers, believing the train damaged, filed out of the cars and down 27 steps to the underpass. Overhead they heard the thunder of a plane.

After a 15-minute wait, the guard called down, "All clear! All clear!"

Miss Wells climbed on board the interurban and went on to Sakuragi-cho, the terminus. From there she strolled along the waterfront of Yokohama to the New Grand Hotel where she met Mr. Normura, the manager.

"I see the Japanese fliers are practicing," Miss Wells said.

"That wasn't Japanese practicing," Normura replied, "it was Americans. It was the real thing."

Yokohama-bound, Lieutenant Bill Bower flew plane 12 about the peninsula in search of checkmarks. Abruptly, a hill loomed dead ahead. Bower gunned the engines and climbed instantly to 2500 feet. The left engine cut out. The bomber foundered. But Bower, discovering the trouble, shoved the mixture controls up. The engine caught.

Pursuits tailed Bower as he moved south, but remained at a respectful distance. Near Sakura, Bower saw the blaze lit by Greening. Opposite Yokosuka, he changed to a westerly course. The plane at ground level shot through a formation of bombers which were landing at an airfield.

The flak increased. One burst tagged the ship. With barrage balloons covering his primary target, the Yokohama shipyards, Bower swung wide and dumped his pay load on the Ogura Oil Refining Plant and a group of factories and warehouses. Curving south, inside the line of balloons, Bower eluded erratic artillery fire from the hills, fire which exploded the balloons. On the withdrawal course, Waldo Bither's .30 caliber pumped away at a power plant and a weather boat in the harbor.

Lieutenant Edgar McElroy's plane, the third part of Greening's element, hit the coast 50 miles off course. Swinging back to sea, he flew along the beach for 20 minutes, overshooting his mark. The bomber, retracing its path, met intermittent fire from the batteries at the mouth of Tokyo Bay. McElroy bore through the ack-ack straight toward his objective, the workshop and building-slip area of the Yokosuka Naval Station. Sergeant Bourgeois, dropping his first bomb, made a chance hit on a minelayer being converted into an aircraft carrier. His other two demolitions exploded at one-and-a-half-second intervals, hitting a large factory building which sprawled over several blocks, blowing up a gigantic crane, firing a ship in her slip. As McElroy's incendiary cluster broke apart over the naval base, the assault on the Tokyo Bay region ended.

The last phase of the raid from the sea began. Those planes assigned to Kobe, Osaka, and Nagoya were approaching Japan. Don Smith in plane 15 had picked up a radio station and enjoyed its musical program for over an hour. As he closed the coastline, he checked the station's position by compass indicators, locating it in Tokyo. Suddenly, an alarm broke up the program. After 45 seconds of ringing, a voice shouted in Japanese. The alarm rang again. The station ceased transmitting.

Smith and Major Hilger, his element leader, flew along

together until they spotted the cliffs at the south end of Boso Peninsula, due east of the Yokosuka Naval Station. Neither had visual contact with the last plane—Lieutenant Farrow's.

The two B-25s shot over small boats below, their occupants standing up, waving. Hilger's gunner, Jake Eierman, squeezed the trigger of his .30 caliber, but it jammed and couldn't be cleared. The skipper ordered Eierman to stay put in the nose and be ready to release the bombs if anything happened to Jim Macia, the bombardier. They all felt hungry, and Sergeant Ed Bain munched a peanut butter and jelly sandwich in the turret. Staring down from the cockpit, Hilger was impressed with the drabness of the Japanese cities.

As the two planes came into the Ise Bay region, Hilger turned north to Nagoya to make his run from north to south across the city. Although Tokyo had been hit an hour before, Hilger met no fighter opposition.

Sergeant Eierman saw a cleaning woman rush out of a door and shake her mop at them. Hilger called out over the intercom, "Look, they've got a ball game on over there. I wonder what the score is."

Antiaircraft batteries flashed. Sergeant Bain sputtered, "Hey, Major, those guns are shooting at *us!*"

Under the impression that the city was larger in area than it actually was, the crew experienced difficulty locating the targets. Landmarks failed to stand out as expected. The river near Nagoya Castle was almost dry and inconspicuous. The large-scale maps did not outline the built-up area of the city. They sighted the towers of the Yasami Radio Station, a mammoth graveyard, and the Nagoya Steam Plant.

Hilger made his run at 1500 feet. Black globs of ack-ack filled the air. Jim Macia dropped his four incendiaries at intervals of one minute, aimed at the military barracks adjacent Nagoya Castle, the Matsuhigecho oil and storage warehouse, the Atsuta Factory of Nagoya Arsenal, and the Mitsubishi Aircraft Works. After the last incendiary clipped off the shackles, Hilger power-dove at two oil tanks, and Bain spattered them with machine gun fire. Eierman noticed that Bain's left fist was clenched, his fingers oozing peanut butter and jelly. As the B-25 left the mouth of the bay, Macia turned and watched a column of smoke with a mushroom head, 6000 feet high, rising from the city.

Don Smith and his crew entered Kobe at its northeast corner. It looked just like the objective folder. They anticipated ack-ack and interceptors but swept in unopposed. Below trains were running as usual and citizens placidly walked the streets.

The bomber flew east along the harbor front. Smith's run at 2000 feet, 240 mph, was businesslike, effective. Squatting in the tiny bombardier's seat, putting his feet in a steady position, bracing his right elbow on his right knee, Lieutenant Howard Sessler checked the drop angle. To Sessler it was essential to sit in the exact same position each time. The drop angle differed as his head moved up and down. His hand was free to use the toggle switch. Over the intercom, he directed Smith toward the objective. Sessler waited for the target to meet the line on the window before releasing the bombs.

Blink. Blink. Blink. Blink. Sessler dropped four incendiaries on dockyards, a steel factory, the Electric Machinery Works, and the Kawasaki Aircraft Factory. The crew craned their necks for a better view.

Selecting a target in Nagoya instead of continuing to

Osaka, Bill Farrow snapped into the intercom, "Get set to drop the bombs at five hundred feet. There is the first target." With the wind howling through the jagged hole, bombardier Jake DeShazer released three incendiaries. The plane twisted and turned. To the left DeShazer saw flames gush from a tank farm. Farrow dodged through a torrent of ack-ack fire. Immediately they were over a factory where DeShazer dropped the last incendiary.

The bomber withdrew, taking evasive action by quick changes of altitude, hugging the valley, rising abruptly to 200 feet, dipping, dipping further, rising, swooping out over the ocean. Bobbing up and down, the pilot of a fishing boat waved frantically with both hands until DeShazer pumped a few rounds from the .30 caliber at him.

One by one all the raiders, except Ski York, headed for the Chinese mainland, leaving behind Tokyo, Yokohama, Kobe, and Nagoya. They were mystified by the weak fighter opposition, the lack of a warning system, the ineffectiveness of antiaircraft fire.

In the mind of every pilot were questioning thoughts, anxious thoughts. Was it possible to make Chuchow with their gas load? They rechecked the gas gauges; sweated the tanks for the long haul, the hard pull down Oshima Strait, down over the East China Sea. They pitted their technical skill and luck against the distance, trying to squeeze extra miles out of the gas.

In the wardrooms of the *Hornet* and *Enterprise,* steaming full speed toward Pearl Harbor, naval aviators wondered if the B-25s would reach Free China. Six hundred fifty miles had been the outside limit of the gas load.

Rehashing the events of the morning, navy personnel praised Captain Mitscher's seamanship and timing at the launch. They agreed the B-25s' take-offs had been ragged and dangerous. Captain Frederick L. Riefkohl, skipper of the cruiser *Vincennes,* believed it was a miracle they all got off. But the fact remained that every bomber was launched without mishap with a heavy load under adverse conditions. In Admiral Halsey's opinion, this reflected credit upon Mitscher and the Army pilots.

That afternoon, all hands waited anxiously for news from Tokyo. An English-speaking propagandist dubbed "Lady Haw Haw" by the *Hornet*'s crew came on the air over radio station JOAK. She chatted on and on in a saccharine voice, interpreting the news, advertising the cherry blossom festival. Unexpectedly, her voice changed to a screech. She shrilled that enemy planes were over Tokyo, flying low, bombing. The radio went dead.

Later in the afternoon, the Japanese made more broadcasts, estimated casualties at 4000, urged citizens to pray for rain, took the line that only hospitals, schools, and non-military targets had been struck, and bragged that nine planes had been shot down.

Task Force 16 was still in hazardous waters. Throughout the long afternoon bluejackets waited for attack. Every few minutes lookouts spotted unidentified aircraft, proving the Japanese were searching. The *Enterprise*'s scouts sighted an enemy patrol plane, which luckily didn't see them. Thirty minutes later, another Japanese plane failed to detect the squadron.

On the *Hornet*'s bridge, lookouts spied two patrol vessels to port. Up went Navy bombers. From a high altitude the planes dove straight at the first ship. Ensign J. C. Butler's 500-lb. bomb hit close aboard the port side causing fragmentary damage. Other planes screamed down upon the patrol craft, their bombs erratically spraying the entire area. Simultaneously, the cruiser *Nashville* closed to within range and let loose. The helter-skelter bombing and the low dives made the cruiser's tactics extremely hazardous. After ten minutes and 167 rounds of ammunition, the *Nashville* saw the first craft sinking. As she was going down, the *Nashville* rescued five of her eleven crew members. The other enemy picket was set afire by an *Enterprise* bomber and apparently sunk. The task force vanished into the vastness of the Pacific.

In his stateroom that evening, Commander Stanhope C. Ring, chief of the *Hornet*'s air group, composed a chanty for the ship's newspaper:

'Twas the eighteenth of April in forty-two
When we waited to hear what Jimmy would do,
    Little did Hiro think that that night
The skies above Tokyo would be alight
    With the fires Jimmy started in Tokyo's dives
To guide to their targets the B-25s.

    One if by land and two if by sea
But if from the air the signal was three
    When all of a sudden from out of the skies
Came a basket of eggs for the little slanteyes
    So Hiro and Tojo just buried their heads
Under the carpets and under the beds.

    Their posteriors turned into rising suns
As bombs they fell by tons and tons
    Then a stab of pain made Hiro shiver
Was it his kidney or was it his liver?
    Or was it perhaps; alack, alas
A returned Jap medal was assaulting his
    (Honorable self) . . . .

It was mid-afternoon when Premier Hideki Tojo

rushed to Tokyo, cutting short his inspection of the Army Aeronautic Communications School. At the Imperial Palace, he was chagrined to learn that he had been preceded by the Home Minister, Foreign Minister, Navy Minister, and five generals, who had offered the Emperor their congratulations on the safety of the Imperial Family.

Citizens of Tokyo were ordered to keep their radios switched on permanently for special instructions. Home Minister Michio Yuzawa went on the air and warned the nation against being caught off guard. "Tokyo and a few districts were visited by enemy air raiders today," he said, "but the damage caused was very slight and no confusion was seen in the affected areas." General Asasaburo Kobayashi, Chief of Staff, Air Defense Headquarters, called the raid a valuable training experience. Mamoru Shigemitsu, Ambassador to China, then on leave, reminisced about his experiences in London when the Nazis bombed the British capital. "Compared with the German raids," he said, "today's air attack cannot be called an air raid."

The newspaper *Nichi Nichi* reported, "The enemy's daring enterprise failed to achieve any results worth mentioning"; *Hochi,* "Their weak attack was a sort of comic play." Military censors were quick to delete the magazine article, "Tokyo Raid," from *Chijinyu,* which accused the air defense command of a shameful performance: "Especially I cannot understand as a layman the fact that they could not protect us from an air raid at *noon.* What is our defense army doing?"

Yasutaro Hani, an inquiring magazine writer, learned of the warning to Tokyo by the *Nitto Maru No. 23.* "Why didn't we know about it even at noon?" he asked. Military censors cut this statement and blue-penciled

Nichi Nichi's reference to a damaged army hospital, a reference considered a bad influence on Japanese morale.

Despite censorship, many Japanese were troubled. "I guess," suggested Mrs. Yukie Kimoto, housewife, "the Americans are laughing at the Japanese defense for being so foolish." Describing the havoc of incendiaries, Kenichi Tada wrote, "A wooden house is a gate of hell. The person in charge of fire prevention is a Saint Joan of Arc. At this moment, if an enemy plane drops a bomb haphazardly, the city will start to burn up."

When Florence Wells returned home that evening, her excited and fearful roommate, Miss Yoshida, detailed the events of the day. Tokyo citizens had run out into the streets to gaze at the sky. The thunder of exploding bombs shocked them into realizing that the capital had experienced its first air raid. "Will it happen again?" inquired Miss Yoshida.

Kazuko Suzuki was in bed with a high fever. Her father, refilling the water buckets, related how a schoolboy of 16 had met violent death. The Suzuki family worried about the oldest daughter who had set out that morning for downtown Tokyo. She hadn't returned by evening.

At the British Embassy, diplomats drank toasts to the American fliers.

The wife of a factory owner returned to her home in Osaka from a family picnic. Neighbors rushed over to describe an American plane's run past the city and to speculate on the damage from its bombs on nearby Kobe. Up until that moment, she had trusted the newspapers' boast that no enemy bomber could ever strike Japan. Now, she was uneasy, wondering what would happen to Osaka if not one but 100 planes came over.

The legal section of the First Demolition Ministry was

already on the job, assessing the damage. It reported 50 deaths, 252 wounded, 90 miscellaneous buildings completely gutted. Destroyed or partially damaged were four electrical companies, one garment factory, six gas tanks, two miscellaneous factories, a food storage warehouse, a naval ammunition dump, a gas company, an army arsenal, six wards of the Nagoya Second Temporary Army Hospital, six elementary or secondary schools, numerous civilian residences, a naval arsenal laboratory, one airfield, the Communication Ministry's transformer station, the National Hemp and Dressing Company, the Japanese Diesel Manufacturing Company, Factory No. 1 of the Japanese Steel Corporation, a warehouse of the Yokohama Manufacturing Company, the Mitsubishi Heavy Industrial Corporation, and the Nagoya Aircraft Factory.

At Kisarazu Air Base, units of the 26th Air Flotilla, which had gone out to attack the task force, returned without locating it. The search continued.

To intercept the American carriers, the Japanese Navy massed 90 carrier fighters, 80 medium bombers, 36 carrier bombers, and two flying boats. The Combined Fleet alerted eleven submarines from various squadrons and deployed the fourth and fifth cruiser divisions of the Second Fleet. The carriers *Akagi, Soryu,* and *Hiryu,* comprising the First Air Fleet, were returning from the Indian Ocean and had reached Bashi Channel south of Formosa on 18 April. They were ordered to hunt and attack Halsey's force.

Japanese propaganda station JOAK broadcast overseas in eight different languages: "The cowardly raiders purposefully avoided industrial centers and the important military establishments, and blindly dumped their incendiaries in a few suburban districts, especially on schools and hospitals."

The broadcast was picked up in Chungking, already the victim of 107 Japanese air raids. Chinese newspapers rushed out extras, and groups gathered devouring the exhilarating news. Movie theaters flashed the report on the screens. Audiences cheered. Shopkeepers and customers forgot business to discuss the news. A gang of illiterate road-building coolies downed tools to listen intently to their boss read an account, supplementing it with explanatory details.

New York Times correspondent Harrison Forman wrote out his dispatch in the din of thousands of firecrackers set off by correspondents in the hotel compound, accompanied by whoops and cheers of scores of Chinese. Chungking's War Minister, Ho Ying-chin, told enthusiastic reporters, "The nightmare of the Japanese militarists can be shattered only by bombs. These raids on Japan proper are only the beginning."

Three hours out of Tokyo, Doc Watson's crew spotted the silhouettes of enemy ships steaming northward. Red tracers floated up. Puffs of smoke rose and raced aft. A pattern of explosions splashed in the sea ahead of the bomber. Sheets of water gushed high in the air. To fly into a geyser would be like ramming a brick wall. "And there I was," Scotty sputtered, "firing back with a .50-caliber machine gun. Might as well have had a cap pistol." But Scott kept firing short bursts and sprayed his tracers in the general direction of a cruiser.

Wires and spars flicked by as Watson roared past, hugging the sea. Every gun on the starboard side of the cruiser let go at him. The propellers fought to hold the plane steady. Watson executed violent evasive maneuvers, half-expecting the wings to fall off. The floating balls of fire still dogged him. A shell burst on the ocean, spraying the windshield with salt water. Banking to the left, he gained altitude and escaped. An hour more to the coastline.

Fortunately, none of the other planes, driving down the East China Sea, were attacked by enemy surface units. For most it was a time of watching the sullen lapping ocean, of staring ahead and seeing nothing except sky and sea, of reading and rereading the gas gauges.

A tail wind suddenly whipped in behind the B-25s. It was the purest luck. Navigators, almost incredulous, exclaimed through the intercoms, "There's a wind coming up, a tail wind!"

"The weather man on the carrier said it couldn't be."

"Tail wind, by Christ, you're right. Sure as hell there is. We've got a chance, by Christ, we have."

This strong wind which blew the bombers across the sea was from the same storm which had prevented Colonel Alexander from alerting the Chinese airfields.

Night was falling. The planes flew into a storm front, a towering barrier, hulking between the sea and the China coast. Pilots plowed through the swirling murk. Rain lashed at the windows. Down drafts slammed the B-25s around. They heaved and quaked and pitched.

Facing zero-zero weather which shrouded the mainland, the mission was up against the reality of making a wheels-up night descent on the churning sea below or, when the gas gave out, parachuting out over the wild terrain of eastern China, close to Japanese lines, perhaps within them.

Colonel Doolittle measured the tail wind, checked the gas gauges, and calculated the distance left. They could never make it to Free China. The rain stopped momentarily. Doolittle looked at the fuel indicator again and decided they might make the coast after all. Every crew member stared straight ahead. Landfall was minutes away. Suddenly there it was. Rain poured down again. The signal from Chuchow for which they all listened did not come.

All planes were groping their way in the solid overcast. Pilots coaxed and wheedled their engines. Some couldn't recognize any landmarks when they crossed the coast. Flying on instruments, others failed to make visual contact at all. None knew except in a general way where they were heading.

Pulling up to 6000 feet, then to 8000 feet, Doolittle went on instruments, staggering in the storm, nursing the engines. Occasionally, he saw dim lights below through a break in the clouds. He and Cole scrutinized the instrument panel.

"We'll have to bail out," Doolittle said conversationally through the interphone. Leonard first, Braemer second, then Potter and Cole. The B-25 circled twice more, then the colonel put the plane on AFCE—Automatic Flight Control Equipment. The right engine gasped.

Quickly, without hesitating, Leonard, Braemer, and Potter jumped. The straps of his parachute entangled with his seat, Cole struggled to free himself. Doolittle untwisted them and slapped Cole on the shoulder as the co-pilot disappeared through the escape hatch.

Shutting off the gasoline, the Little Man leaped into the blackness.

ESCAPE

ALL THROUGH THE NIGHT, OBSERVANT CHINESE
saw plane crashes and fires blaze on the mountains' sides.
Huge white phantoms floated earthward, swinging from
side to side in the wind and rain. Strange-looking men
stumbled down from the slopes and sputtered an inco-
herent phrase. The Chinese took these foreigners, who
had landed bruised and shaken, into their huts and fed
them and, later, guided them onwards. Already word
went swiftly from mouth to mouth, village to village,
"These men are friends. Bring them to Chuchow."

The stories of the aviators are remarkably similar. No
man refused to jump. They jackknifed into the night.
Though their adventures differ in detail, all but three
crews, employing Yankee ingenuity, made themselves
understood and received food and shelter.

One American sergeant, wandering about that night,
stumbled upon a Chinese couple, who brought him home,
fed him and shared their only bed. The sergeant was too
beat to care when the man performed his husbandly
duties. "If they did not mind my presence," he remarked

during debriefing, "I sure as hell didn't care, just so they didn't keep me awake."

Most of the parachutists landed close to the fringes of Japanese-occupied territory. The country folk of East China and the guerilla chieftains operating in this zone accepted the Americans. Unhesitatingly, they risked their lives by conveying them to safety. No token of friendship was denied. The Chinese gave of their slender stores, never asking for recompense.

The Japanese position in China enveloped the coastal ports and islands of Chekiang Province. From the city of Hangchow, the enemy held a line running northwest through Kiangsu to the Yangtze River. They dominated the greater part of the valley, so that the line of occupation ran west, dipped southward, following the irregular course of the Yangtze west.

It was 2331 hours when Sergeant Fred Braemer leaped from Doolittle's plane. His chute jerked open, spun violently, winding the shroud lines to within a few feet of the chute. Braemer, twisting and turning, clawed the lines apart to prevent more spinning. His gun-belt snapped loose and fell away into the night.

He bounced on the side of a steep hill. He couldn't see in the blackness. Unbuckling his chute, Braemer crawled 20 feet down the hill and got no place; he crept 20 feet up the hill, past his chute, and found nothing. He came back to his chute, cut a section from the shroud lines, rolled up in it, slung his left arm around a bamboo tree, and fell asleep.

Hank Potter went tramping through a field toward a point where he had detected lights on his way down. He didn't find them, so he, too, curled up under a tree and slept. Sergeant Leonard spent the night wrapped up in his parachute. Lieutenant Cole, falling into a pine tree, shinnied down, stretched his chute between it and another tree, making a hammock, and proceeded to go to sleep.

Doolittle's descent was smooth until he sank to his knees in a wet, soggy rice paddy. Splashing out, soaked and freezing, he noticed lights 100 yards away. He shrugged out of his chute and sloshed down the road in the rain to a farmhouse. Doolittle, banging on the door, hollered *Lushu hoo megwa fugi, Lushu hoo megwa fugi.* A bolt slammed into place on the other side. Lights blinked out. Doolittle continued to rattle and shout. The door remained bolted.

He wandered down a road and stumbled upon a large crate, covered with planks, on two sawhorses. To gain protection from the biting wind, Doolittle threw off the boards, mounted one of the sawhorses, jumped into the crate, and discovered a dead Chinese, hands folded peacefully on his chest. The colonel was in the local morgue. He had no scruples about staying the night with a dead man, but the box wasn't wind- or rainproof. Abandoning the coffin, Doolittle struck out up the road.

It rained harder. In a decrepit water mill, he escaped from the storm, but the dull cold wrapped and hugged him tight, seeping through his clothes.

Trav Hoover's crew sighted the islands and peninsulas jutting out from the China coast. Hoover started to climb above the overcast. The right engine was fine. The left coughed and cut out. The plane staggered, exhausted, half-dead. Turning on the booster pumps, Hoover lowered the nose of the bomber and veered sharply to avoid crashing into the coastal islands. The left engine picked up again. Hoover jockeyed the engines. Pilot and co-pilot inspected the instrument dials for signs of relapse. Trav started to climb again. The left engine gasped and stuttered. Hoover dove and, with the gasoline running from rear tanks to the forward outlet, the engine barked alive. The crew labored to resuscitate the B-25. At any moment the left engine might crack. With desperate zeal, Hoover tried "one damn thing after another" in an effort to lift the aircraft.

For the third time, Hoover put the ship into a climb. Again the left engine stalled. With the gas gauge indicators bumping the bottom, Hoover decided to make a wheels-up landing and started searching for a runway. Through the window he spotted a flat stretch of rice paddies along the edge of a bay.

It was raining and growing dark. Hoover buzzed the landing place twice, and made his approach. Co-pilot William Fitzhugh watched the pressures and temperatures and began calling off the decreasing air speeds. Hoover ordered flaps. Fitzhugh lowered them, and the pilot with gentle touches adjusted the trim tabs. They were going to make it. It was going to be just like any other wheels-up landing.

The rice paddies came up, a quarter of a mile in front, and they were letting down to them. The B-25 dragged forward and down. Hoover cut the ignition switches before the bomber hit the ground. The ship settled easily. The crew was unscathed. Abandoning the aircraft, they packed off guns, knives, flashlights, pocket compasses, canteens, emergency rations, and extra clothes.

With the crew standing 200 yards away, Sergeant Radney fired the incendiary pellet on the turret tanks. It failed to ignite. Hoover ran back and set fire to the engines. A sheet of flame engulfed the plane.

Behind them in the darkness, they heard a babble of

U.S. Air Force photo

Maj. Gen. (then Lt. Col.) James H. (Jimmy) Doolittle wires a Japanese medal to the fin of a 500 lb. bomb which shortly thereafter was returned to its Japanese makers in a blast of destruction.

Marc A. Mitscher, *(right)* commander of aircraft carrier *Hornet* at time of raid on Tokyo.

Below: Fleet Admiral C. W. Nimitz *(right)* and Admiral William F. Halsey.

National Archives

Official U.S. Navy photo

Official U.S. Navy photo

Planes stored on carrier before raid.

Official U.S. Navy photo

Planes readying for take-off.

U.S. Air Force photo

The starter "hits the deck" as the B-25 gathers speed down the flight deck of the *Hornet*.

U.S. Air Force photo

Roaring off into a gray sky, B-25 heads for Japan.

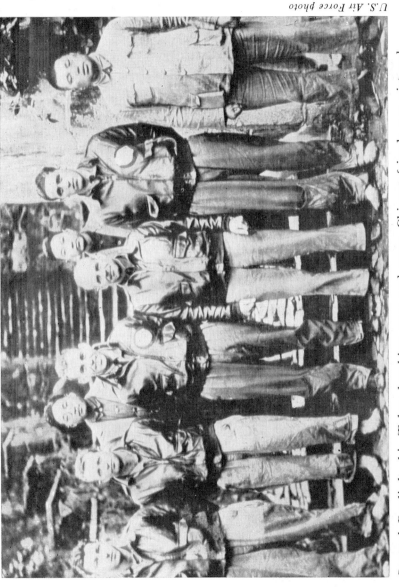

U.S. Air Force photo

General Doolittle, his Tokyo bombing crew and some Chinese friends are pictured in China after the flyers bailed out following the raid on Tokyo. *Left to right:* Staff Sgt. F. A. Braemer, bombardier; Staff Sgt. P. J. Leonard, engineer-gunner; unidentified Chinese; First Lt. R. E. Cole, copilot; General Doolittle, pilot; unidentified Chinese; First Lt. H. A. Potter, navigator; unidentified Chinese.

Front page of the English language newspaper Osaka *Mainichi*, 19 April 1942, reporting the attack.

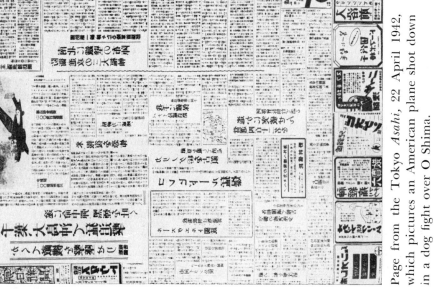

Page from the Tokyo *Asahi*, 22 April 1942, which pictures an American plane shot down in a dog fight over O Shima.

Reg Manning in the Arizona Republic, Henry E. Huntington Lib.

Two cartoons expressing American reaction to Tokyo raid.

The Milwaukee Journal & Ross A. Lewis, Henry E. Huntington Lib.

U.S. Air Force photo

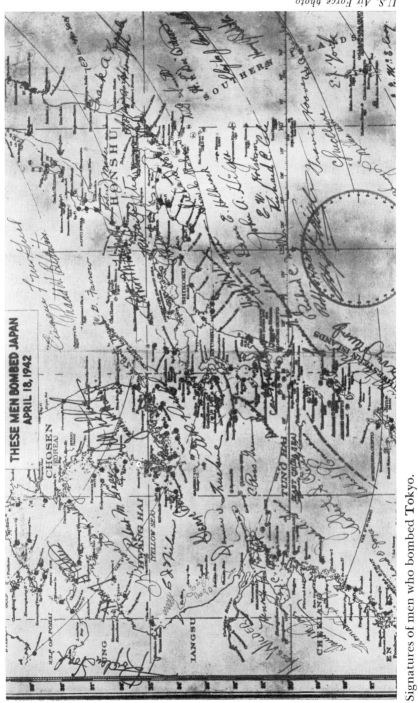

Signatures of men who bombed Tokyo.

voices, high-pitched voices. The chattering came closer. Uncertain whether this was Japanese-occupied territory, the Americans junked their luggage and dogtrotted west through the rice fields up the first mountain. They paused momentarily; glanced back. There in the night, the pursuers stood silhouetted against the flames. On the mountain the airmen huddled together in a trench and shivered in the rain until morning.

Sergeant Aden Jones, Gray's bombardier in plane 3, pulled the release, kicked the door, and bailed out through the forward hatch, followed immediately by Charlie Ozuk, the navigator. Shorty Manch flashed the light in the rear to see if Corporal Lee Faktor had gone. Seeing no one, he called "all clear" to Gray.

Manch stood six-foot-six and weighed 240 lbs. In addition to being a crack pilot, he had two hobbies—music and guns. Before leaving the *Hornet,* he had slipped his portable phonograph and his carbine rifle into the plane.

Now, looking like a banana-republic revolutionist with two .45s, one Luger, and a small pistol strapped around him, and cradling the phonograph in one arm and the carbine in the other, Manch jumped.

When all the crew had left the plane, Gray switched on the gyro-pilot and dove at 6200 feet.

Sergeant Jones lay on his back, ten feet from the top of a mountain. He heard another plane pass overhead and, since he could see nothing, he dug in his heels so he would not slide down and went to sleep.

Ozuk, after a short descent of 800 feet, struck the 5000-foot peak. His chute caught in a tree, crushing him against a rock ledge. He lay there injured, his left leg badly cut. In bandaging it, he knocked a piece from his shinbone. He hung from the chute that night and desperately struggled to cut himself loose.

Corporal Faktor's first jump was his last. He perished on a Chinese hillside.

Manch's was a rough descent. He did a three-quarter flip and "let'er bust." The jolt of the chute opening made him see red, and yanked off all the guns except for one .45. He crash-landed on the side of a hill, tumbled for 70 feet before coming to a stop. He sat there and surveyed his possessions. All that remained was the .45 and the handle of his phonograph still clutched in his left hand.

Brick Holstrom in plane 4 listened to the radio but couldn't distinguish Japanese from Chinese. Red danger lights glowed on the instrument panel. The gas was gone.

At 2342 hours the crew bailed out. They all hit the side of a Chinese mountain and remained there until morning.

Davey Jones flew on into the blackness, past his ETA for Chuchow, hoping to find a break in the overcast. Failing, Jones turned 180°, wobbled back, and prepared to abandon ship. The crew hurriedly rehearsed the Chinese words meaning "I am an American."

The gunner and bombardier dove out almost together, followed by the navigator. Co-pilot "Hoss" Wilder went to the forward escape hatch and snapped on his gun belt. Putting the plane on gyro-pilot, Jones scrambled back into the navigator's well and joined Wilder. The two passed a bottle of whiskey.

Buckling on his gun belt, wrapping the strap of his musette bag around his left arm, Jones watched Wilder let himself down and drop out. He followed. The crew of plane 5 all landed safely in Free China.

Dean Hallmark ran out of gas before he reached the

coast near Ningpo. Both engines died. Plane 6 pulled up, shuddered, and flattened out. Hallmark checked the altimeter and speed. Air speed was already down and falling. He issued orders to the crew, watching his height and his speed at the same time. Whitecaps studded the ocean as he put the nose down. His speed was lower than he would have liked, and the sea seemed to come up towards him at an angle.

The ocean rushed up fast and, after the first bumping, they knew something was wrong. The left wing, smashing the water first, was severed. The fuselage was split open all the way down. It was a wild, frenzied scene. Hallmark was jolted violently through the windshield. Water gushed into the ship, full force. Corporal Donald Fitzmaurice, still in his turret, went straight down, deep, struggled free, and swam up. The waves were so fierce that the wreckage bounced like a gigantic yo-yo, up and down. Expecting the twisted pile of steel to sink immediately, they all jumped into the bitterly cold water.

Somehow the crew clawed their way to the life raft. It collapsed instantly. Their Mae Wests worked perfectly.

Terribly shaken up by the crash, Sergeant Bill Dieter and Fitzmaurice flailed around. The other three, sticking together, started swimming toward shore. Lieutenant Bob Meder, the co-pilot, glanced back and saw Dieter and Fitzmaurice slowly submerging. Splashing back he helped Fitzmaurice. The other two airmen, churning toward the beach, were unaware of the difficulty. After four hours in the water, Nielsen and Hallmark made shore at different points. They walked a few steps, then sank in exhaustion.

Meder eventually dragged Fitzmaurice's limp body to the beach. After collapsing in the sand, he finally staggered up the coast. To his horror Dieter's body lay face down, washing back and forth in the breakers. The tide had brought him in faster than Meder could swim with the corporal. Fitzmaurice was dead, too.

Ted Lawson had already decided to save the aircraft by landing on a stretch of rugged, sandy beach instead of heading inland. If they could, the aviators would spend the night in the B-25, take off at dawn, and fly on to Chuchow in the daylight. Lawson had 100 gallons of fuel left.

Rain spattered the windshield as he made the approach. His wheels were down. The flaps were down. The plane was gliding in for a normal slow landing. Lawson was judging it by inches, for the beach was narrow. Suddenly, the engines cut out. Lawson hit both throttles, frantically trying to snap the engines to life. The wheels touched an onrushing breaker, bigger than the rest. They hit it going 140 mph.

The shock was tremendous. Lawson and co-pilot Dean Davenport shot upward through the glass, plastic and metal windshield, seats, and all. Bob Clever went through the transparent, metal-braced nose, head first. Charles McClure lay in agony inside the plane. In the turret, Thatcher was unconscious.

The crumpled plane was sinking. They were almost completely under the sea with water racing in from all directions. Lawson found himself sitting in his seat in the sand, underwater. Unfastening his safety belt, he floated upward with the help of his Mae West. In the crash the dioxide capsule had broken and inflated the life jacket. Along with Clever, Davenport, and McClure, he was washed ashore. They were all terribly injured. Lawson was "bashed open," Davenport recalled, "his whole face seemed to be smashed." McClure's face was a red mask of blood. Davenport was cut severely. Clever couldn't walk.

When Thatcher regained conciousness, he saw water plummeting through the top of the turret which, he thought, was the rear escape hatch. He was dimly aware of trying and trying but not getting anywhere. He was upside down. Still dazed he yanked at his Mae West, and, finally orienting himself, groped his way to the rear hatch and escaped. He grappled up to the belly of the plane. On shore he saw the four officers. In the dark and rain, Thatcher splashed through the combers to reach them.

Just then two peasants came running down through the rocks. Thatcher pulled out his .45 and took aim. Lawson yelled for him not to shoot.

Were they Chinese or Japanese? It was too dark to study them closely. Six more jumped down from the rocks. Cautiously, silently, they inspected the aviators. One turned, tapped his chest, and mumbled, *Chinga.*

The Americans were in Chinese hands.

The peasants started jabbering away. The crew blurted out *Lushu hoo megwa fugi.* Excitedly, in sign language, the Chinese inquired whether any more airmen were in the plane. Assured there were none, they started helping the battered Americans to a thatched hut a half mile away. When two peasants grabbed McClure under the armpits, he screamed in pain. They dropped him. McClure, struggling up by himself, tried walking. He had smashed into Lawson's seat, and he believed his two arms were broken.

Inside the hovel amid the moans of the injured, Corporal Thatcher assessed the condition of the wounded. His heart turned over when he saw Lawson, who was lying on his back with his legs stretched out. At first it was impossible to tell where the shreds of his saturated coveralls ended and the ragged flesh began. The left leg was hopelessly shattered. Thatcher saw a vicious deep cut, just above the knee and a gash between the knee and ankle, so deep that he could see the white bone running inside the gory scarlet flow behind the twitching fibers of muscle.

Lawson was in a stupor from loss of blood and shock. By now the blood had coagulated inside the wounds, and Thatcher simply bandaged them with his handkerchief and gauze from the small first-aid kit attached to his gun belt.

There was no morphine, no protection for Lawson against pain but the numbing shock of the gaping wounds themselves. Lawson watched him steadily, saying nothing, as he wrapped the cuts, working with skill and composure. Lawson did not stop bleeding completely.

Stunned at how waxen and ghastly the bare leg looked, Thatcher continued to check the injuries. The foot below the left ankle was so badly bruised that it was starting to turn black. Thatcher tenderly inspected two deep scratches on Lawson's chin and counted nine front teeth missing.

The corporal feared the pilot would die or gangrene would start in his leg before they reached a hospital. "If gangrene had set in, I wouldn't have known what it was because I don't know what it's like."

He nursed the others. Clever's hips and back were so badly sprained he couldn't stand up to walk. All he could do was crawl on his hands and knees. His head was caked with so much blood he couldn't see. Thatcher decided to leave it that way rather than wash it, as there was danger of starting infection with unsterile water. Infection, thought Thatcher, would set in soon enough anyway.

Davenport had severe cuts on his right leg between the

knee and ankle. McClure's most serious injury was two dislocated shoulders, which were horribly swollen clear to the elbows. He could not move his hands or bear to lie down, and had to sit up all night.

One Chinese hovered over Lawson. Pointing to the gashes in his left leg, the pilot made a sewing motion over the cuts. The peasant shook his head, but called to another. Lawson again went through the motions. Again they shook their heads. They had no sewing equipment.

Thatcher took a lantern, walked down the path to the beach to remove the large first-aid kit from the plane's tail. But the tide had come in. He went back to the hut.

Suddenly the door burst open. Another Chinese entered, went to each airman, inspecting the wounds, examining all the buttons and insignia on their jackets, then whispered to the others. The peasants encircled Thatcher, making him understand by gestures that Japanese patrols were searching for Americans, and for him to run for it. Thatcher glanced at Lawson, Davenport, Clever, and McClure, groaning piteously on the dirty bamboo mats. He shook his head. He'd stay.

It was a night of hell for the injured.

Striking a course for Vladivostok 600 miles away, York throttled back to save gas. Poring over the maps of the Russian coast, Herndon discovered them not too accurate or detailed. The afternoon waned. York and Emmens divvied up a candy bar. Slowly the crew made out land in the distance, tall mountains looming out of the sea. York climbed and, three miles out, swung right and flew north along the shoreline. Up in the cockpit behind the pilots, Herndon unfolded his map and pointed to their approximate position, 40 miles north of Vladivostok.

Verifying this position by outstanding features of the

terrain, York turned 180° and headed down the coast, this time nearer to shore. The Americans encountered no antiaircraft fire, no pursuits. They cut inland. As they swerved, York and Emmens sighted off to the left the jut of land extending seaward.

"Jesus, look," exclaimed York. Looking out the windows, the Americans saw a gigantic airfield with 40 orange-winged aircraft.

"Let's get the hell out of here," York snapped.

The plane turned, lowered, picked up speed, roaring out across a ridge of hills, down through a wide, flat valley, flashing past tumble-down buildings and strangely-dressed men. York and Emmens suddenly sighted a plane beneath a camouflage netting close to a building.

"Hell, it's an airport!" York hollered. Below the natives waved and pointed out the direction to land.

The B-25 began its approach. Emmens lowered the flaps all the way. There was a slight jolt, then the tail was down, and the tail-skid was bouncing. Emmens raised the wing flaps. The brakes were screeching. The plane slowed to taxiing speed. Emmens was already unhooking his safety belt as he spotted the black-coated soldiers. York maneuvered the bomber around to face an open field. Emmens pulled the flaps the rest of the way up and locked the brakes. The engines stopped. Pilot and co-pilot cut the switches. The plane was silent. Not a word was spoken. Just off the right wing, wearing their round, flat caps, the welcoming party clustered and inspected the aircraft, grinning. Plane 8 was in Russia.

The quiet and shy sergeant, Eddie Horton, Joyce's gunner in plane 10, had sat hour after hour on the long flight to China in the worst position of all—aft, in the un-lighted fuselage—separated from the crew with nothing to think about except how he had nearly died a dozen times when his ship had been hit by antiaircraft fire and attacked by enemy fighters. Over the interphone he heard Joyce saying the plane was already over a rough, mountainous district of China. Possibly, they would all have to jump. Horton looked out his little window again. All he could see was the driving rain.

The weather was zero-zero when the bomber neared the Chuchow ETA. Joyce realized a landing was impossible. The ship slowed to 125 mph and went up to 9000 feet.

"Crew from pilot—crew from pilot." In his steady, easy, midwestern voice, Joyce told his men, "I figure that we will be out of gas in less than 15 minutes, so it looks like we will have to bail out. Horton, you first, then Larkin, then Sally [Crouch], then Stork. Larkin, you wait 'till Horton is gone before you release the forward door—it might hit him. O.K. fellows, I'll see you in Chuchow. Let me know when you're ready, Horton."

There was a pause. Then Joyce heard a break in the rhythm of the noise. That meant the rear hatch was open.

"Horton to pilot—all ready, sir."

"Go ahead, Eddie, and good luck to you."

Without hesitation, Horton said, "O.K. lieutenant, here I go, and thanks for a swell ride."

Joyce called to him again. Silence. Without a moment's pause, Horton had stepped out into the night over the wilds of an unknown land.

To Joyce, Horton's spirit exemplified the spirit of his whole crew. None was afraid to jump, but they were all bitterly disappointed they had to abandon the aircraft instead of touching down safely and completing their mission 100 per cent.

The last to dive, Joyce rolled the stabilizer back to

keep the plane from gaining too much speed, and waddled around the cockpit with his chute on. He encountered trouble squeezing between the armor plate back of the seats while, at the same time, pushing the stick forward to keep the ship from stalling. At the escape hatch in the navigator's well, clutching food and equipment, he leaped.

It was pouring rain. Joyce pulled the ripcord. The chute opened, but the leg-strap buckles malfunctioned, almost flipping him out. The chest strap gave him a stunning blow and shook his pistol out of the shoulder holster into space. He swung wildly, corkscrewing slowly earthward. Below him the plane hurtled into a mountain, exploded, burst into flames. Seconds later, Joyce pitched onto a steep slope. Uninjured, he hustled out of his chute, wrapped himself up and, like the others of his crew, tried to get a little shut-eye.

Doc Watson watched the red lights on the instrument panel. The plane was flying on fumes. They'd never make Chuchow. Watson climbed to 10,000 feet, put the ship on AFCE, picked a heading for Kian. Assembling the crew and explaining the situation, Watson told them to gather their equipment for bailing out. Silently, they waited. The left engine quit first. Watson lowered the landing gear and gave the order to jump. Four airmen plunged out in quick succession, landing easily on a mountain side.

Trimming the aircraft, Watson turned toward the navigator's well and forward escape hatch, but his web belt, canteen, pistol, seat-type parachute were tangled in the armor plate. The right engine stopped. Cursing, struggling, Watson finally wrenched free and tumbled through the hatch.

His chute popped open. The shock and pain were

terrific. Watson's right arm was fouled in the shroud lines. He tried pulling it down. He couldn't. Laboriously with his left hand, he untangled the mess. His right arm dropped loose, dangling, dislocated. Watson crash-landed. He was out cold, face up, in a mountain stream.

Bill Bower read "zero-zero-zero-zero" on the gas gauges of plane 12. He called his men on the intercom. Sergeant Waldo Bither, the bombardier, crawling from the nose to the navigator's well, snagged his ripcord and accidently opened his chute. He continued on to the escape hatch, where he calmly repacked it. When his turn came, he leaped out, the chute working perfectly.

As Bither floated down, he yelled to locate his comrades. Faintly, he heard someone call out, but, in the fog, he was never sure of his direction. Bither struck the steep grade of a mountain, relaxed, uninjured. In the first awful moments of disorientation, he decided to smoke a cigarette. He stood quietly and listened for a signal from one of the others. He heard nothing. His smoke finished, he flicked the stub away. Dumbfounded, Bither watched the tiny glow disappear out into space, falling, falling, falling. The sergeant was on the edge of a ten-foot ledge. He clutched the hillside and waited for daylight.

McElroy's crew collected around the forward hatch. They shook hands and jumped—there wasn't anything more to do. Lieutenant Knobloch, the co-pilot, lit in an open field. Shouting on the way down, he received no answers, but saw a flashlight shining as he bumped to earth. He flicked on his light. He got so many answers, he ceased blinking, and started walking toward the lights. They could not be reached in the dark. Off to the left he detected a village. After a few paces, he stopped and decided to wait until morning. It might be Japanese. At 0300 hours he saw a single light. He answered. It was McElroy.

Grabbing the emergency handle, kicking the door of plane 11 open, Sergeant Mel Gardner, Greening's gunner, saw only space, fog, and rain. "It was now or never," he recalled. He oozed out into the slip stream. For two seconds nothing happened. Suddenly, all of Gardner's breath was knocked out of him and he was snapped around to a sudden stop. He seemed to be floating sideways, not downward.

While descending, Gardner began looking for the ground with his flashlight. He fell with a thud and tumbled head over heels twice before stopping, spraining both ankles. He halted on a mountain side, just short of the edge of a bluff, which dropped off 20 feet straight down. After resting, he forced himself up the mountain where he snuggled into a niche for the night, rolled up in his chute.

Greening, who bailed out last, took two armfuls of groceries with him besides his gun and flashlight. Not until he had fallen 500 feet did he grapple with the problem of jerking the ripcord without dropping his load. Quickly, he chose the flashlight and gun, dumping the groceries out over eastern China. Flashing his light on the way down, he spotted others blinking back.

Co-pilot Ken Reddy bruised his left knee and gashed his head in landing. Slowly he took a swig of water from his canteen, dressed his wound with first-aid bandages, pulled himself up the shroud lines, and freed himself from the chute. Whipping out his knife and slashing the lines, carrying the silk with him, Reddy stumbled down the mountain, yelling all the way. No one answered. He decided to bed down, but all attempts to build a fire with wet wood failed. Unable to sleep, he again tried to descend the mountain until it became too hazardous. Finally, he lay down in his chute, constructing a small shelter. It was raining hard when he fired one shot from his pistol. No one replied.

Jake Eierman, Hilger's gunner, salvaging his pint of whiskey but leaving behind fifteen cartons of cigarettes, stood at the escape hatch. It looked awfully deep and black. Eierman hesitated, wondering if he should go head first or feet first. Jumping out feet first, striking his head against the rear of the hatch, he was dazed momentarily. When he came to, the chute was open. He lit his flash. There was nothing but air and fog. Just before landing, he blinked his light again and saw water below. For an instant Eierman thought it was the ocean, but it was a rice paddy with a running stream. He hit and unbuckled his chute quickly. After slogging two miles, he came to a settlement. All the doors were barred. His knocking went unanswered. He was wet, cold, miserable.

It seemed hours before Eierman located a man and his wife and persuaded them, by sign language, that they had nothing to fear. These simple folk led Eierman to their cottage, next to a temple, and called out the whole family. A wobbly old man took charge, offering the sergeant food, but Eierman stuck to his own canteen and emergency rations.

When Hilger jumped at 8500 feet the gas gauges still registered 50 gallons and the plane was running perfectly. Hilger had been in the air 13 hours and five minutes and had flown a distance of almost 2300 miles.

Jolted when his chute ripped open, he fought to recover consciousness. He discovered his musette bag gone with all his rations, matches, and whiskey. The gun and canteen were still secure. Excruciating pain shot through his left groin. In pawing his way between the armor plate he had accidentally unhitched his right leg strap. This resulted in his slipping further down in his harness, the breast strap belting him, then slapping him in the nose, causing it to bleed.

Hilger, floating earthward, saw a hole in the fog, steered for it, and hit it square. But it was not a hole. With a breath-taking, spine-jarring crash, Hilger slammed into a peak. When he came to, he was lying on a 45° slope with his chute snarled in the trees. Rain poured down. With no flashlight, Hilger decided to stay put for the night. Despite his horribly sprained left hand and his wrenched back, he sliced his chute down and crawled up to a shelf on the slope. He spread the silk over two bushes, crept beneath, and went to sleep.

In plane 15, Don Smith crossed the Chinese coast 25 minutes ahead of his ETA and only ten miles off his planned landfall. Directly ahead Smith caught sight of a huge mountain sticking out of the clouds. He banked right, increased the throttles, so he could climb, turned due east, and headed back out to sea.

Smith had every bit of emergency power pouring into the two engines. The temperatures were up as high as they could go, the pressures were too high. The right engine began missing a beat here and there. The left engine was backfiring.

Smith and Griff Williams, the co-pilot, studied the gas gauges and did some figuring. They decided to ditch in the sea.

Smith ordered everybody into their Mae Wests. They still had 500 feet, but the water looked close. The waves were not bad. The glide held at 120 mph until a few feet off the surface of the sea. They were paralleling the coast, 400 feet off shore. Cutting back on the throttle, Smith tried to hold it off as long as possible. Williams put the flaps down and, by watching the distance between propeller tips and the water, Smith was able to hold it off until he had slowed down to 90 mph. Just before hitting the water, Smith cut the throttles; Williams, the switches.

"Stand by for water landing," Smith barked. He fastened his safety belt. He opened his window for better visibility. Williams' was open.

Smith eased the plane down gently into the swells with such flawless skill that not one of the crew suffered the slightest bruise.

Water rushed through the smashed nose, swirling into the pilot's compartment at seat level. Smith shattered the glass above the navigator's well and grabbed for the equipment, but gas masks hung near the window, and he had to pull them out of the way before he reached anything of value.

The wings rested on the waves. Williams, Smith, and Sessler wrestled out of the top escape hatch onto the wings, their orange Mae Wests dangling limp around their necks and waists.

Aft in the plane, Sergeant Ed Saylor had made the mistake of donning his winter flying coat just as the plane struck the sea. When the aircraft stopped, he removed the hatch, but, with the turret tank installed, he couldn't inch by with the bulky coat. He tore it off as water burst through the hatch, forcing him to dive and swim back up.

Doc White, also aft, was sitting up to his shoulders in muddy, cold water. He hustled to the escape hatch and helped Sergeant Saylor. White could tell by the way the bomber rode the waves that it wasn't going to plunge to the bottom immediately. He rummaged about, searching for equipment that might be useful to the crew, rescuing his emergency kit and gun, which he passed to the boys outside.

Williams yelled to the doctor to get out. The plane was slowly settling, the wings were awash, the life raft sliding back and forth against the fuselage. All the crew were out. The landing lights remained on. The aviators stuffed their parachutes, gun belts, rations, and first-aid kit into the raft. The B-25 was sinking, the tail rising, the nose dipping. They took their places in the raft and shoved away just before the bomber went under.

All five sat in the rubber dinghy with their elbows and legs pressed so close together that if one moved he'd knock the next guy into the water. Waves washed over them and, occasionally, dumped one of them back into the sea.

The coastline was vivid. They headed toward a break in the cliffs, paddling, splashing. Gradually one end of the rubber raft softened, but they couldn't locate the leak in the darkness. The left end collapsed. The raft rolled over, pitching the airmen and their precious cargo into the surf. The rations, guns, and surgical kit shot to the bottom. Wallowing in the waves, they scrambled back on board the half-inflated raft and continued stroking toward the beach. Sessler had had enough of the raft. He dove into the water, swam toward shore in his Mae West, and was soon out of sight.

Bucking the current, the other aviators were not making headway. They changed course and steered toward a point which they could barely see in the gloom. Forced

128

to battle through breakers up to nearly vertical cliffs, they strove to save the raft. Lacking the muscle to hoist it up the steep slope, they tied it to a rock.

Atop the cliffs, the Americans, wet, exhausted, and worried about Sessler, plodded across a field toward a dim light in the distance. Their total armament consisted of a sheath knife and a pocket knife. They found a hay-stack, a goat pen, and a tumble-down farmhouse. The light went off. The bolt shot home. They banged and hollered the Chinese phrase, "I am an American." Silence. Finally, they crawled into the goat pen which was filthy but dry.

After an interval, the farmer stepped out of the house holding a lantern, peering and motioning them inside. The Americans watched their host build a fire with rice straw on the floor and, warming their water-soaked bodies, saw his wife and mother dish up hot food from an ingenious-looking stove. The smoke almost suffocated the airmen, but the victuals revived them quickly.

The entire village was pushing and elbowing their way into the hut to stare at the foreign curiosities. They had never seen a white man. The Americans endeavored to make them understand who they were by drawing pictures of flags and making signs. They made no head-way. Fretting about Sessler, Doc White stuck up four fingers and pointed to the four aviators. The villagers understood. The doctor then showed a fifth finger, in-dicating that one of them was missing. Again they nod-ded. A man left the crowd to look for Sessler.

Children exhibited a paper-back almanac, containing four English words across the top of each page with their Chinese equivalents. White, flipping the pages, struck upon the word for America. With this page and more sign language, they identified themselves.

By means of an American map, the Yanks figured out

where they were. They had waded ashore on the only island in the entire group which did not possess a permanent Japanese garrison. The aviators explained they must get to Free China quickly. The Chinese controlled one of the two lighthouses close by and promised to guide them there the following night. Here they would be picked up by launch. After much gesticulating, the villagers left, and the crew fell asleep.

Bad luck dogged the last plane with Farrow and his crew. The murk was so thick they had no idea what part of China they were over. Farrow circled a town, called on the radio, and frantically searched for runway lights. The gas tanks registered empty. Farrow shouted through the intercom, "We gotta jump."

Corporal Jake DeShazer stuck his legs out of the hatch. The wind was shrieking. He gave a shove and watched the bomber go past overhead. DeShazer, hauling on the ripcord, felt the welcome jerk as his chute opened. The sound of the plane's motors died out. The fog was thick around him. The corporal bounced with a terrible jolt into a Chinese cemetery.

He was thankful to be on solid ground. Despite the shooting pain from two fractured ribs, he was able to stand. He held his .45 high in the air and fired twice. No answer. DeShazer cut off a portion of his parachute to shield his head from the rain and trudged off. Drifting about for hours, he finally came to a brick building, entered, and sank in exhaustion.

Lieutenant George Barr, Farrow's navigator, his knee viciously bruised, wobbled around in the night. Suddenly he froze in his tracks. A Japanese sentry stepped out of the darkness. He was grinning.

Barr was taken prisoner and marched to Nanchang,

his hands bound tight behind his back. Pushed into Military Police headquarters, the Japanese methodically questioned him and offered him strong drink and "some sweet stuff." Barr answered with name, rank, serial number. The interpreter shoved him roughly around the room. After a half-hour's interrogation, the questions stopped, and Barr dropped on a cot and fell asleep.

At 0100 hours that night Tatsuo Kumano, private first class in the Japanese 18th Army, was awakened by a comrade and informed that sentries had caught an American flier. Military headquarters in Nanchang needed Kumano immediately as an interpreter. At 0130 hours, soldiers ushered Kumano into a room where intelligence officers were pumping Sergeant Harold A. Spatz, Farrow's gunner. The questioning continued. Spatz answered softly with no tinge of anger. Name, rank, serial number. Over and over, hour after hour, intelligence officers grilled the prisoner without result.

After the inquisitors quit for the night, Spatz chatted unofficially with Kumano about his home town in Kansas, his family, his schooling. Kumano learned that the sergeant had left San Diego on a ship, which took him to an island in the Pacific, where bombers were lined up on a temporary landing strip. He and his compatriots had taken off from that runway and traveled due south for seven hours.

By dawn of 19 April, 15 of the 16 bombers had been abandoned either over the wilds of the Chinese interior or along the seacoast of northeast Chekiang Province. Eight of these crews descended in the general vicinity of the designated airfields. Two bombers flew much farther into China. Five terminated their mission in the coastal region adjacent to Hangchow, which lay within Japanese lines. Their burned, broken, and downed planes lay scattered across 400 miles of Chinese land and water. The 16th B-25 made a routine landing at Vladivostok.

Fortunately, a 30-knot tail wind had picked them up and blown them across the East China Sea. Most had reached the mainland with gas to spare. The 15 had ventured as far as they dared until disaster would have been the price of further flight.

They had not been schooled in the techniques of abandoning ships and parachute descent. The crowded interior arrangements of the B-25 were not conducive to easy departure. Few of the aviators knew enough about bailing out to secure equipment to their persons before dropping from the ship.

The crews' orders were to make for Chuchow. In mountains, in rice paddies, in villages, along shores, the Americans spent a restless night.

The dawn of 19 April was overcast. Fagged out from doing knee bends most of the night to keep warm, Doolittle walked down a road and encountered an aged Chinese farmer. The peasant, gawking at the mud-caked colonel, remained motionless. Doolittle sketched pictures of a railroad train. The farmer beamed and led the colonel a mile up the road to Chinese military headquarters.

Greeted by a major who spoke English, Doolittle spelled out that he was an American, an ally to the Chinese, and had jumped out of a bomber during the night along with four others. The major and three of his men, clutching their tommy guns with obvious disbelief, were silent. It registered in Doolittle's mind they were planning to shoot him on the spot.

He suggested leading the soldiers to his parachute.

The major was willing. Guiding them up the road, past the water mill, the coffin, the house with the bolted door, they finally came upon the rice paddy and located the place where Doolittle had landed.

The chute was gone. The soldiers, still cradling their tommy guns, said something in Chinese. Doolittle insisted the major interrogate the peasants at the farmhouse. Surely, they'd recall his knocking. At the hut the major shot questions at the farmer and his wife. The peasants appeared dumbfounded. No plane had flown over the house. Nobody had banged on the door. No parachute had been found. The American was lying.

Doolittle was adamant. He was a colonel in the United States Army Air Corps. He had bombed Japan. Four other men had parachuted out of the plane.

Unexpectedly, two soldiers who were searching the hut strode out, the parachute in their arms. The major's suspicions evaporated; he pumped Doolittle's hand, commanded his men to rustle up some food, ordered another soldier to return to headquarters and turn out a patrol to search for the other airmen.

That same day co-pilot Dick Cole was picked up and escorted to Tien Moo Shan and was soon sipping tea with Doolittle. A dispatch went out to Hap Arnold.

Sergeant Paul Leonard awoke that morning and walked up the valley in search of the colonel. He roamed about, skirting villages, as he wasn't sure whether he was in enemy territory. Suddenly, Leonard was ambushed by four rifle-toting, angry-looking men. One motioned for him to raise his hands. The other three cocked their rifles and took aim. Leonard whipped out his .45, fired blindly, and then he turned and tore up the mountain. He watched groups of men gathering at the foot of the hill. They all had rifles. Crouching in a crag, hiding himself the best he could, he calculated a course for escape that night.

Navigator Hank Potter walked into a village. The citizens treated him well until Sergeant Braemer straggled in. The villagers confiscated their guns, knives, and rations. Potter whispered to Braemer, "Let's get out of here." They legged it out of town, the natives right behind them. A half-mile farther on, the peasants caught them and took their money and watches.

Potter and Braemer continued west and ran across a lad shouting, "Me China boy! Me China boy!" He led them to his hut where they rendezvoused with a guerilla chieftain.

It was 1300 hours when Sergeant Leonard peeked out of his hiding place. He saw the crowd. At its front were two mud-spattered men in Air Corps togs. They were distinctly American. Leonard squinted again. It was Potter and Braemer!

Figuring they were in enemy hands, he grimly reloaded his clip, yelled, and ran down the mountain, ready to shoot it out with their captors. To his embarrassment, he discovered they were in friendly hands. Soon Doolittle's crew was reassembled at Tien Moo Shan.

The colonel wished to inspect the wreckage of his B-25. There was equipment to be destroyed or salvaged. Halfway up a hill 12 miles from the village, Doolittle and Leonard located the totally demolished plane. One engine had been ripped off and lay in the gully amid the rocks, completely smashed. Scavengers of the neighborhood had methodically sacked the plane. Everything worth carrying off had vanished.

His eyes searching the junk pile, Doolittle despaired. The entire mission had been a fiasco. The other 15 crews were probably in enemy hands or dead. Their planes lay smoldering on the mountains or sinking in the sea. "It's been a complete failure," he said to Leonard.

"Damn it, Paul," he snapped, "they'll never give me another plane. They'll ground me from now on, and I'll be lucky if they don't break me."

Leonard assured him that when they finally reached the States, the colonel would be wearing the star of a general and a Congressional Medal of Honor.

They started back, but darkness overtook them. Their Chinese escort located a farmhouse where they spent the night on the floor. Doolittle awoke, startled by odd noises, gruff and low. Reaching up, drugged with sleep, he touched sharp bristles and, quickly, the sounds changed to frightful squeals. He had pre-empted the bed of the family pig.

Trav Hoover and his crew, after their forced landing in a rice paddy, slept in a trench. In the morning they moved into a nearby pillbox on the top of the mountain. They hid all day. Between them, they had one tin of field rations, three candy bars, a full canteen of water. At nightfall they hiked westward. Traveling in the darkness was arduous. The irrigated rice paddies and the hills retarded their progress. They slogged along until past midnight before bedding down on the side of a mountain without protection from the rain. They struck out again at dawn.

All day they trudged up and down, hiding from farmers, avoiding villages. They were exhausted, discouraged, begrimed. That night they built a lean-to out of grass and spent the night in the mountains. The airmen pushed westward the next day. Late in the afternoon they chanced contacting a farmer for food, certain they could not last much longer without it. As the farmer's son watched curiously, Hoover drew a Chinese flag and a Japanese flag on the edge of his map. The boy understood and traced the enemy line, indicating they were in free territory.

They started down the road once more, deciding their only choice was to follow the well-worn paths and risk detection. Armed guerillas jumped them, robbed them of everything except their clothes, and marched them into the village of Son Ah. Frantically by sign language, pictures, and pidgin English, the Americans made them understand their plight. The guerillas relented and returned all their equipment except their .45s and, next morning, sent them across the bay in a boat guarded by armed ruffians.

By boat, rickshaw, train, sedan chair, and foot, Hoover's crew kept working westward toward Chuchow. Along the way they met a Chinese aeronautical engineer, T. S. Liu, who had escaped from Shanghai disguised as a wealthy merchant. Liu, speaking English fairly well, traveled along with Hoover the rest of the way, acting as interpreter, making all the arrangements. They reached Chuchow on 29 April, 10 days later.

Charlie Ozuk, Bob Gray's navigator, hung limp in his parachute all night and all the succeeding day before he regained enough strength to cut himself loose. Bandaging his badly-cut leg, fashioning a makeshift cane, he hobbled westward. His progress through the hills proceeded at a snail's pace. On the afternoon of 20 April, he contacted friendly Chinese who fed him and put him up for the night. Too beat to go further, Ozuk was resting in a hut when a lone soldier entered, and exhibited a letter in English. He was Chinese and had orders to lead survivors to Chuchow.

The first person co-pilot Manch encountered was a woman carrying a bundle of sticks. "Pardon me, madam," he said by way of introduction. The woman appeared not to hear. Manch drew closer and drawled, "Lady." She took one look at his six-foot-six frame and ran shrieking into her house, slamming the door. Manch knocked. No answer. He pushed on the door. It opened. The room was empty. Peering through the back door, he saw the entire village fast disappearing into a bamboo thicket. Finally a Chinese, whose curiosity exceeded his fear, approached and sketched a Japanese flag. Holding his nose, Manch shoved the picture away. The Chinese grinned. He then brought out a four-year-old copy of *The Saturday Evening Post* with a cover picture of President Franklin D. Roosevelt. Manch beamed, pointed to the president, then to himself. The Chinese laughed, and they shook hands.

The next morning, peasants made signs and noises like an airplane hitting a mountain. Manch set out with them and, at noon, discovered his B-25 sprayed across the terrain. It had been stripped. The Chinese led Manch to a village, where he found pieces of baggage, clothes, navigational equipment, and the body of Corporal Leland Faktor.

Gray's bombardier, Sergeant Jones, awoke at dawn and searched for his comrades, firing off his .45. Following a mountain stream, he stumbled upon a village, where he spent the night. The next day he plodded on until a Chinese soldier handed him a note from Gray. Joining up with the skipper and Manch, Jones was borne in a sedan chair westward toward safety.

Pilot Brick Holstrom was investigating three huts at the head of a stream, when, suddenly, brigands surrounded him. They led him into a hovel and insisted he strip naked. Once undressed, Holstrom noticed the Chinese rifling through the pockets of his uniform. Out on the porch, everything was gone from his gun belt but the water canteen.

He slept in the hut all night. In the morning he dressed and started off bereft of watch, knife, gloves, silk scarf, first-aid packet, billfold, and compass.

A peasant guided him down the trail to the village of Ken Chi. From then on, it was all routine. At Chuchow he was reunited with his crew.

At daybreak, Captain Jones was walking west. He came upon Chinese peasants and, after drawing a picture of a locomotive, he was given general directions. Reaching the Shetsung depot, 18 miles east of Yushan, he bumped into his co-pilot, Hoss Wilder. Together they corralled a hand-car from the stationmaster and set off. Eight miles out they were stopped, escorted onto a special train, and steamed triumphantly into Yushan, where the multitude gave them a thunderous reception. Already the crowd had learned of the "great deed of the brave American heroes." At the airport, the citizens washed their feet, cleaned their uniforms, fed them royally, and put them to bed. They resumed their journey that afternoon for Chuchow, where they rejoined the rest of the crew—Manske, True-love, and McGurl.

When plane 6's navigator, Chase Nielsen, spent by his four-hour swim, opened his eyes, the fog was full on his face. Off to the left he noticed two vultures on a rock looking down at him and wryly chuckled. With enormous effort he got up and staggered off along a path.

Pilot Dean Hallmark, injured in the crash, remained

on the beach until dawn. Stiff but able to walk, he stumbled upon the same track taken by Nielsen which wound around the coast to a fishing village. Chinese guerillas stationed there took the bedraggled Hallmark into a stinking mud hut and gave him tea. Waving a wad of currency, by signs and gestures, Hallmark beseeched them to guide him to safety.

One Chinese suddenly indicated someone was coming. Hallmark, thinking the guerilla was warning him of Japanese, picked up a club, jumped to the side of the door, and raised the weapon over his head.

The door opened slowly. It was Nielsen. Later co-pilot Bob Meder, also hurt in the smashup, was led in. Fitzmaurice and Dieter, he said, lay dead in the sand.

For three days, the fliers waited impatiently at the garrison. They wanted to escape over the mountain passes and renewed attempts to pay the guerillas, but the Chinese refused to venture out, insisting the enemy had sentries on all the trails. The Americans then sought to employ sampans to run down the coast. Suddenly everything was wrong.

Miss Cora Houston, an American Methodist missionary, stared frozen in disbelief at a patrol of Japanese soldiers swinging down the path toward her mission station. They forced the door and ransacked the place. That night she learned that three American airmen had been betrayed. The enraged villagers uncovered the informer and swiftly beheaded him. Heroic attempts by guerillas to rescue the Americans were thwarted by the Japanese. It was two months before Miss Houston knew that the captured aviators had bombed Tokyo.

At dawn, Corporal Dave Thatcher checked his injured companions in the peasants' hut, then hurried off to the beach and wrecked plane, hoping to salvage the first-aid kit and morphine. But he was too late. During the night the tide had washed the bomber ashore. The engines, torn loose in the crash, still rolled in the breakers. The nose, a mangled mass, was stove in clear back to the bomb bay. Thatcher stood on the sand fascinated by the sight of scores of Chinese carting off bits and pieces. Three ran away laden with aluminum tubing. One toted a wheel with part of the landing gear. Thatcher noted the outlines of a Japanese surface vessel far out to sea. The Americans had crashed near Nantien, a Chinese village on an island off the coast, about 150 miles due south of Shanghai.

There at Nantien, a guerilla, "Me, Charlie," indicated in pidgin English that Japanese patrols were only a third of a mile away. Thatcher wanted to get started for the mainland, safety, and a hospital. That afternoon the four wounded men wrapped in blankets on stretchers were lugged by coolies accompanied by Thatcher and guerillas. They hiked through high mountain passes to the other side of the island and a waiting river boat. After boarding the flat-bottomed craft poled by Chinese, they moved down a dirty canal. The only sound was the thump of the pole against the back of the skiff.

Dave Thatcher methodically went from Lawson to Clever to McClure to Davenport, laboring to keep the four officers alive. He pushed himself to the limit. A 19-year-old kid, he had had thrust upon him the responsibility of bringing to safety four critically injured friends.

At 1830 hours, the boatman maneuvered the craft toward two steep dykes. Eight fresh coolies appeared, scrambled down to the boat, nimbly picked up the stretchers, and started up the dyke. At the top the Americans could glimpse the mainland of China off to the westward. The coolies carried the injured on the ridge of the dyke, then down along the edge of a ditch, paralleling the shore, to a waiting junk.

Suddenly the coolies dropped the stretchers in the ditch, jarring the wounded, who screamed in pain. The guerillas flattened out and gestured for silence. They peeked out over the embankment.

A Japanese gunboat loomed up offshore. The Americans watched the craft slide up against the junk and listened to the interrogation. The patrol vessel pulled away. Waiting impatiently until it was out of sight, the coolies grabbed the stretchers. Dashing across the beach with the injured, they waded through the water and helped them into the junk. Quickly the guerillas jumped in behind, their guns ready for action. The junk slipped away to the mainland and Sanmen in Free China.

Dr. Chen, director of the hospital at Linhai, wondered why there had been so many air-raid alarms. The first one had come on the night of 18 April.

On the afternoon of the 21st, the local magistrate rushed into the hospital with an urgent telephone message from Sanmen, requesting medical aid. Four American airmen lay wounded in the village. Dr. Chen and an assistant hurriedly left Linhai. Twelve hours later they located the fliers in a dingy room at the magistrate's headquarters. Without hospital facilities, Dr. Chen and his associate merely redressed the wounds and made arrangements with authorities to transport Lawson and his crew to the Linhai hospital. Meanwhile Thatcher sent a telegram to Chungking describing their condition.

When the little party left the following morning in sedan chairs, the citizenry of Sanmen with their band gave them a tumultuous send off. They had been the first Americans ever to visit the village.

At Linhai, missionaries of the China Inland Mission helped the aviators by mending and washing their uniforms. Dr. Chen performed minor surgical procedures on Lawson, enlarging the wound of the left knee, removing loose fragments of patella, extracting loose teeth. Lawson responded to Dr. Chen's questions by opening and closing his eyes. He could not eat, and nurses fed him intravenously.

The meal lasted from 1000 hours until 1300 hours. Ski York, Bob Emmens, and the others along with the Russian colonel and his staff toasted Roosevelt and Stalin, the armies, the air forces, airmen everywhere, victory, Roosevelt and Stalin. The table groaned beneath caviar, cheeses, pickled fish, black bread. Plates and glasses were filled and refilled. The toasting ended, the main meal began: cream soup, roast goose, fried potatoes, roast young pig whole, and a hot, sweet chocolate drink.

Talk ran from the war and B-25s to Russian air force heroes and America's pioneers in aviation. Two Russians entered the dining room clutching the fliers' life-preserver vests. The colonel curiously tugged at the strings, inflated one of the Mae Wests. The vests and carbon dioxide capsules were handed around the table.

Late in the afternoon, the Americans, as they climbed on board a DC-3, glimpsed for the last time their B-25 parked in the distance. The Russian plane streaked down the runway, took off, circled the field, and traveled north, sweeping up a valley. The Americans speculated upon their destination. Several of them optimistically believed they were heading for the States. The Soviets had seemed hospitable, but there was always the possibility of being turned over to the Japanese at some airfield in Manchuria.

Early that evening, the DC-3 let down at an airport where, off to one side, stood groups of pursuit planes. In the distance, the Yanks noticed numerous buildings with twinkling lights indicating this was a good-sized city. Just as the party left the DC-3, the Russian colonel turned and said, "Khabarovsk." The name didn't register with the Americans.

As they walked briskly toward waiting limousines, they were surprised to discover that all the fighters lining the field were dummies. Crammed into automobiles, they were whisked off to a drab-looking building on the rim of the airport. Inside a long room behind a heavy desk loomed a hulking ape of a man in a Russian general's uniform. Other officers and a pasty-faced woman clustered about him. This, whispered the interpreter, was General Stern, commander of the Far Eastern Soviet Army.

During the half hour's questioning as to targets, number of aircraft, routes taken, the Americans avoided implicating the *Hornet* and Task Force 16. After the interrogation finished, the general arose. The governments of the United States and the Soviet Union had reached a decision. The fliers were to be interned.

It was foggy when Lieutenant Dick Joyce awoke. When the mist cleared, he hiked over the crest of a mountain. Chinese were already picking in the wreckage of plane 10, which was spewed up and down the slope for miles. Hailing the peasants, making them understand he was an American, Joyce was guided to a village, then passed on from town to town until he reached Chuchow. Like his crew, he reached safety without incident.

Wet, cold, Doc Watson lay alone in pain. His right arm hung useless. He jammed a morphine ampule in with his left hand, wincing from the pin prick. Then, slipping out of his parachute, cutting a sling from the silk, sure that his two .45s were in order, he followed a stream. He wandered a mile and more. Around the bend of the creek, he saw peasants in the valley below wading about in the rice paddies. Watson remembered Jurika's instructions on distinguishing Chinese from Japanese. The Chinese were tall, slender, always grinning; the Japanese, short, squat, and rarely smiled. The American watched, confused, aching, numb from the cold. Fifty per cent were squat, 50% were tall. He wished he could glimpse their expressions. Weighing the odds, Watson decided to gamble and walked down the path, shouting, "I am an American" in faulty Chinese.

The peasants froze. Slowly one of them, "Charlie," as Watson later nicknamed him, grinned, nodded, and motioned. They led him into a hovel, where they dried his soaking clothes, wrapped him in a blanket, and fed him hot water and rice. Drugged from the morphine, Watson slept for 18 hours, until Monday morning, 20 April.

He bade farewell to his friends that afternoon and set off down the path for another village. Here he located a mission station and orphanage. A Chinese, who spoke English, kept repeating, "You friend safe, you friend safe." The headman cranked an antiquated telephone and, after yelling and screaming for 15 minutes, got the call through. Watson picked up the receiver. "Hello, Doc, how are you?" It was Tom Griffin, his navigator. The boys were safe.

Bill Bower's bombardier, Sergeant Waldo Bither, started a hazardous descent down the mountain trail. As he approached a village, a man watched him nervously. Bither strode up and bowed. The Chinese, returning the greeting, grinned broadly, invited the sergeant into his shack, and offered him food. Bither, taking one look, refused politely, but asked for hot tea instead. While gulping it down, Bither noticed another peasant slip in. He pointed to Bither's flight jacket, stuck up two fingers, and pointed down the trail. The sergeant, leaving immediately, saw footprints made by American shoes on the path. A short distance away, he found Thadd Blanton and Bill Pound and returned with them to the village. Pound pulled out a map with names in Chinese and English. The peasants showed them where they were— 15 miles from Chuchow. Thanking them for their help, the three Yanks struck out. They gradually wound their way around the mountains, heading north. That night a Chinese, bearing a note from Bower, guided them to a village, where they met the lieutenant. A soldier reported that Sergeant Duquette, the remaining member of the crew, had fractured his ankle and was being carried in by sedan chair.

Sighting a wild pheasant, Sergeant Williams of McElroy's crew, laid down a barrage with his .45. He built a fire, roasted his kill, and enjoyed a hearty breakfast. After a short hike, he found the rest of his crew.

Frank Kappeler, Ross Greening's navigator, contacted some Chinese who couldn't understand him, but they led him to a house farther down the hill. Here they fed him and exhibited a book containing a few English words and their Chinese equivalents. The pattern repeated itself. Kappeler, Greening, and the rest of their crew were escorted into Chuchow.

Jack Hilger awakened. The wind had died down and,

to his horror, he heard what sounded like ocean breakers. Had the rest of his crew landed in the sea? Hilger, remembering he'd seen two life jackets near the hatch when he bailed out, was haunted by the thought that some of his men had drowned. At dawn through the scattering, thinning mist, the major was relieved to see a valley below and a stream which had given the illusion of surf.

In the valley nestled a village. He headed for it. The major was completely disoriented, but he hoped he wasn't in enemy territory. When he first encountered the villagers, he could see only a large encircling arc of people, half-mooned about him, dressed in greys, browns, and blues, rags and woolens, heads covered with old towels, shawls, handkerchiefs. He decided to play it by ear. The leader stepped forward—an old movie stereotype with the scraggly moustache and black cloak. He hadn't the foggiest notion who Hilger was, but his gestures and wide grin indicated to the major he was in friendly hands.

Hilger politely refused their food, but desperately tried to make them understand he wanted a telephone or train. After much hand waving and sound effects, one boy nodded and, with the major in tow, started out for a telephone. At each village along the way, the lad proudly displayed his American.

A truck bounced down the narrow road with a load of soldiers in search of Japanese paratroopers. They leaped out of the vehicle at the sight of the major and the boy, gabbling in Chinese. Their tommy guns trained on Hilger. The youngster jumped in front of the American, shielding him, and spoke rapidly. The officer's eye suddenly detected the insignia on Hilger's jacket. He smiled. Relief flooded through Hilger. With pictures, gestures, and grunts, Hilger indicated where his men should be and urged them to organize search patrols. Only then did he leave for the barracks.

After a rest and a meal of pastries—Hilger discovered later they had a dog-meat base—he was escorted to the walled town of Kwang Feng, ten miles away. A high wall soared around the entire city with pagodas at the gates. He jolted down the cobblestone streets in a rickshaw. Peddlers chanted their wares; peanut vendors hawked at the corners; rickshaw men yelled to attract passersby. Here in this strange Chinese setting, the major found Jack Sims, Jim Macia, and Jake Eierman. Down the narrow, alley-like streets marched an impromptu parade. The Americans moved through the town toward their quarters, greeted by the entire population.

At 1800 hours the fliers had their first hearty repast since the raid—fried eggs, meat, vegetables, rice, and a drink concocted of boiling water and canned milk. During the night Sergeant Ed Bain walked in. Hilger's crew was complete.

On that leaden morning, a swarming influx of visitors startled Don Smith and his crew from a deep sleep. One of the group, better dressed than the rest, his nose mostly eaten away by disease, minutely inspected the Americans, their clothing, their belongings. He then vanished through the door. Their host informed them by gestures that the boss had departed by boat to seek help. Fearing betrayal, the airmen were anxious to clear the area. They hustled into their still-soggy clothes and, after breakfasting on rice, greens, and shrimp, departed, accompanied by several Chinese.

They found Howard Sessler, who had slept the night in a cave two miles from where they had splashed ashore. The party tramped to a high point on the island, where

147

their host showed them the surrounding islands and mainland. There was an enemy gunboat in those waters, so it would be impossible, he said, for them to travel during the daylight hours. The airmen decided to go back to the village and stay hidden until evening. Back at the shack, the boss had returned with news. The Japanese had overrun the last lighthouse on the island. If the fliers had headed there the first night, their capture would have been certain. During the afternoon, Smith and his men napped, dried their clothes, and readied themselves for the escape.

At dusk they moved out, cautiously, with five Chinese, to a junk secreted in a cove below the village. Saying goodbye to their friends, they flattened out in the bottom of the boat and covered themselves with mats. The junk headed for sea. It was cold. The intermittent rain became a drizzle. Waterlogged, cramped, lying in the bilge, they glumly watched a Chinese scull the junk. Several times boats passed close aboard. Once they heard motors and, in the distance, saw searchlights.

At midnight, they slid into an island, a much larger one, and tied up to a stone pier. Guided by two Chinese holding paper lanterns high overhead, they sneaked down the quay to a building. After a short confab, the guards permitted the Americans and their guides to pass. They plodded along narrow trails, which zigzagged around rice paddies, along the sides of hills, through deep crevices. The blackness was relieved only by the blinking lanterns. The only noise they heard was frogs' croaking and their own footsteps. It was a long harrowing trek.

They were worn out when they straggled into a farmhouse. After a lot of palaver in Chinese, the guerillas introduced the fliers to their chief, a former cabin boy on a United States merchant ship. He spoke halting English.

Another plane had crash-landed on his island, most of the crew painfully injured. They had left just two hours previously for the mainland. The chief passed around odds and ends the aviators had given him. One card had Davenport's name on it. It was Lawson's crew. The Americans wanted to join the wounded, but the chief shook his head. It was impossible to proceed farther that night. They would sail to the mainland the next evening.

During the next two hours, the Yanks sat drinking and talking with the guerillas. The chief was curious about the bombing of Tokyo and was eager to learn if they had salvaged any machine guns from the plane. The Americans learned that five planes had been heard over the island. One had circled and dropped two flares.

All the next day, the 20th, they hid from Japanese patrols sent out from the island garrison. Five guerillas guarded the Americans. The fliers were amazed at their collection of antiquated firearms—English, French, Belgian, and German pistols, decrepit rifles, and an array of bullets that defied description. Half of the cartridges failed to fit the guns, and the Americans doubted if any of them would fire.

Scouts burst in and reported the enemy coming. The Japanese had fallen upon Lawson's smashed plane and were hunting down the crew. Splitting up helter-skelter, the guerillas and fliers melted into the hills. Once the alarm subsided, they reassembled near a canal, where the airmen boarded a flat-bottomed skiff. They said goodbye and set off down the canal.

At sunset, reaching the end of the waterway, they disembarked and walked to a barrack-type structure, where they dined on eggs, rice, shrimp, tea, washed down with 180 proof wine, which nearly cauterized their throats.

That night they started again. They walked two miles along a sandy beach to an abandoned house. Here they waited for the moon to set before boarding a junk which ferried them across the lake. They got out, clambered up a steep mountain trail to a Taoist temple. The priest, wearing a black gown, puffing on a long pipe which he also used as a cane, addressed a few words to the idols, then brought out the jumping sticks and told the fliers' fortunes.

After snacking on eggs and tea, the Americans lay down on the temple floor and fell asleep. They spent the next day inside the temple. When they motioned to go outside, the guards shook their heads violently. The Americans broke open their rations and handed the priest and guerillas chocolate and, they in turn, brought out sticky, black candy.

A Chinese darted up the trail, waving his hands, gibbering excitedly. Eighty-five Japanese soldiers were marching for the temple. With their obsolete weapons, the guerillas were in no position to fight it out. The Americans were quickly and silently herded down a trail to a farmhouse. While guides and farmer argued, the fliers fidgeted. The Japanese closed in. After what seemed hours, the heated discussion broke up. The farmer showed them into the back room, pushed a panel, and pointed to a secret passageway. They crept down this tunnel to a cave. The hide-out had been carved for just such an occasion. The guerillas lighted a candle. The Americans and Chinese listened in that flickering darkness. A half hour slipped by. A racket outside broke the silence—sounds of scuffling, then screams. The Japanese were thrashing the villagers.

Chain smoking cigarettes, the guerillas in the cave checked their guns, cocked them, and stood, backs flush against the wall, covering the opening. They listened to footsteps of the Japanese, who were pushing into the house which hid the entrance. Two hours of suspense were ended by a yell. The guerillas relaxed. Their pursuers had gone. Fliers and guards wormed out of the cave. The priest met them and, by gestures, reported how he had cried, torn his hair, wrung his hands, and sworn his innocence. The thwarted Japanese had desecrated the temple, defiled the idols, and beat the priest.

The party started off again that afternoon and hiked along narrow trails for eight miles, skirting rice paddies, until they reached a pier and boarded a junk. There was no moon as they headed for the mainland. To avoid detection by a patrol boat, whose running lights they could see clearly, they ducked behind a small island. The junk finally reached the mainland and safety.

It was raining on 24 April when Smith and his crew rode into Linhai in sedan chairs, past ranks of Boy and Girl Scouts, past the eyes of the curious. At the chief magistrate's headquarters, Doc White broke away from the festivities and went directly to the hospital. Six days after the accident, both Lawson and Davenport were in horrible shape. They had lost considerable weight and were on the downhill grade.

Lawson's worst wound was the deep cut in his left leg, extending from two inches above his knee diagonally downward and inward. All the lacerations, major and minor, were frightfully infected. Lawson's entire leg was puffed up and exuded a foul, watery discharge. White then examined the area of dry gangrene. Lawson was delirious.

Davenport's deep lacerations on his right leg were infected. McClure's shoulders were dislocated. Clever had a skull fracture.

White immediately ransacked the hospital. Supplies were short. He located some Japanese sulfanilamide, but doubted its potency.

The doctor inspected and redressed the wounds, started Lawson and Davenport on sulfa, and improved the drainage in Lawson's lacerations. For McClure's shoulders, White rigged up a table over his bed so he could rest his arms, and improvised a splint for his left wrist to prevent contractures.

White fired off a telegram to Chungking for medical supplies. That same day Linhai received a wire from Major Hilger, urging White to locate and bury the bodies of two airmen at a nearby village. The Linhai authorities had no knowledge of the bodies, but reported that several Americans had been captured by the enemy.

Corporal Jake DeShazer, bombardier on plane 16, Farrow's plane, awoke at daylight, stumbled out of the brick building onto a road, and started walking westward. Here and there he met Chinese, but DeShazer thought it odd no one exhibited excitement or curiosity. Occasionally, he stopped them to find out whether he was in enemy territory. No one answered. Locating a store in a village, the corporal boldly strode in and scribbled a few words on a pad. The shopkeeper shook his head. DeShazer continued on, meeting farmers, wandering through villages, watching children wading in the mud along with the squealing pigs.

In the distance he saw a military base. From behind cover, he observed soldiers washing their uniforms in a ditch. But DeShazer couldn't distinguish Chinese from Japanese, friend from foe. He decided against walking into the camp, so he continued on up the road.

Hungry, dog-tired, DeShazer chanced going into a

shack. Two soldiers were playing with children. They glanced up. In pidgin English DeShazer mumbled, "America," and pointed to himself. Then, motioning to the enlisted men, he asked, "Japan or China?"

"China," they replied.

They kept on joshing the children, seemingly uninterested in the American. DeShazer had misgivings. Inching toward the door, he stealthily fixed his .45 so a bullet was in the chamber, hammer drawn back.

He swung open the outside door. Ten soldiers packing rifles, bayonets, and swords blocked the entrance. DeShazer hollered "China or Japan?" He clutched his pistol.

"China!"

Perhaps they were Chinese, reasoned DeShazer, and it would be foolhardy to start shooting at allies. The soldiers shook hands, patted him on the back, and escorted him down the road to camp.

Suddenly, the corporal felt the prick of bayonets in his back. Ten muzzles were leveled at him. The officer-in-charge relieved him of his .45.

Inside headquarters DeShazer sat at a table. An interpreter, speaking fairly good English, pumped him for information. Again and again, DeShazer, deadpanned, repeated, "I don't know," "I won't tell."

Cooks carried in hot cakes and tea. When the American finished eating, the officer said, "You are in the hands of the Japanese." For the first time, DeShazer thought of the chilling awfulness of what could happen.

Lieutenant George Barr awoke in Military Police headquarters and was astonished to find co-pilot Bobby Hite sleeping across the room on another cot. Barr looked out the window and saw the Nipponese snapping pictures of the rest of the crew, DeShazer, Farrow, Spatz.

Without mistreating the five Americans, the enemy demanded information. The airmen resisted. They lingered all day in headquarters then, at dusk, were whisked to an airstrip where they boarded a plane. At Nanking, the Japanese clamped them into solitary confinement—the cells were bare except for a wooden box which served as a toilet. Heavily-armed guards moved back and forth in the corridor.

Here the treatment of the prisoners was barbaric. Handcuffed and blindfolded, Lieutenant Barr was dragged from his cell. "Where do you come from?" "Where do you come from?" When he refused to answer, five enlisted men brutally struck him with fists. They forced Barr to the floor and tortured him with "the water cure." Barr's arms and legs were stretched out, one guard holding each limb. Another soldier wrapped a towel around Barr's face, then proceeded to pour water on it until the prisoner, choking, strangling, was almost unconscious. They let him up and, once he caught his breath, they started over. "Where do you come from?" "Where do you come from?"

Beaten and exhausted, he was led back to his cell. Barr caught a fleeting glimpse of DeShazer in another room. Japanese had placed pencils between his fingers and were squeezing his knuckles.

They continued to grill the blindfolded and handcuffed DeShazer. "I won't talk," the corporal gritted out. More questions. Soldiers came up close to his face, opened their mouths, and laughed hideously. Guards ushered the corporal into another room and untied his blindfold. There behind a table stood a stocky Japanese, smoking a cigar, rubbing his hands. His Mongolian eyes squinted at DeShazer. "I am the kindest judge in China," he said through an interpreter, "I want to treat you real good. Everywhere I have the reputation of being the kindest judge in all China."

They sat down. The judge rifled through papers, stopped, and said sharply, "How do you pronounce H-O-R-N-E-T?"

"Hornet," the corporal shot back.

"And that was the aircraft carrier you flew off to bomb Japan, isn't it?"

DeShazer was poker-faced, silent.

"Colonel Doolittle was your commanding officer, wasn't he?"

DeShazer didn't know.

The judge smashed the table with his fist. "When you speak," he exploded, "look me straight in the eye!"

The interpreter indicated that in Japan it was deemed a high honor for judges to chop off their prisoners' heads. Looking sternly at DeShazer, the judge explained he'd have the honor of executing the corporal at sunrise.

Sarcastically, bitingly, his eyes raging, DeShazer retorted it would be a great honor for himself if "the kindest judge in all China" would confer that kindness upon him. The room rocked with laughter.

By 21 April, the five Americans were on a plane for Tokyo.

On that same day, Lieutenants Hallmark, Nielsen, and Meder, the three survivors of plane 6, handcuffed, leg-cuffed, and bound so tightly at the elbows that their circulation was impaired, were imprisoned on a boat under way for Shanghai. Guards untied the prisoners during the day but, at night, they snapped on the handcuffs and leg irons.

At Shanghai, the shackled Americans were hustled to a building at the edge of an airfield. Both Hallmark and

Meder were so crippled from the crash they could barely hobble. When the three frustrated the Japanese by refusing to answer questions, enlisted men forced them into chairs, tied their hands and legs, then slapped and kicked them about the face and shins.

"Where do you come from?" "Are you Army personnel?" "What are you doing in China?"

The Americans answered. "Lieutenant Robert J. Meder, Serial Number 0-421280."

"Lieutenant Dean E. Hallmark, Serial Number 0-421081."

"Lieutenant Chase J. Nielsen, 0-419938."

Their tormentors taunted them by explaining that they were in enemy hands, and no one in the United States would ever know their fate. If anything happened to them, like execution, they would just be listed as "Missing in Action."

Repeatedly, the Americans replied with name, rank, serial number. The irate Japanese pushed the prisoners to the floor for the infamous water cure.

They still held out. Guards then brought in hefty bamboo poles and held them directly behind the prisoners' knees. Forced to squat, the already partially-lame Hallmark, Nielsen, and Meder winced as guards held their arms while others jumped up and down on their thighs. The Japanese probed and questioned relentlessly. The airmen, red-eyed, crazed, edgy from lack of sleep, repeated their names, ranks, serial numbers. Soldiers manhandled Hallmark onto a rack. With each turn of the lever, Hallmark felt as if his limbs were being torn off, but he continued to refuse to answer their questions.

Sundown came. The Japanese stopped the physical torture, but threatened execution. The jailers started to lead the blindfolded prisoners outside. The fliers wobbled, the pain in their legs was excruciating. Before they collapsed, guards grabbed them under their arms and marched them down a gravel path. Still blindfolded, they heard squads of soldiers marching and drilling. The aviators and their escorts stopped as one group filed up and halted. Nielsen heard rifle butts hit the ground. This, he thought, was the execution site. After a short conference between officers, an interpreter stepped up and said, "We are the Knights of the Bushido of the Order of the Rising Sun; we don't execute at sundown; we execute at sunrise."

The Yanks, relieved that they were still alive, were led back to their cells. An interpreter grilled them. Blindfolds were taken off, but not the handcuffs. From a peg on the wall in Nielsen's cell, guards suspended him by his handcuffs, his toes barely touching the floor.

The next thing he remembered, the sun was coming up, and the jailers were taking him down. His legs pained and, when his arms fell from the peg, he thought they'd drop off.

Rumors trickled into Chuchow concerning the whereabouts of Hallmark and Farrow. Hallmark's bomber had crashed in the sea 75 miles north of Shanghai. Two of his crew had perished. The other three, badly injured in the smashup, had been captured on 21 April. One of these airmen was bayoneted resisting arrest, but not killed.

There was little news of Farrow's crew. From refugees pouring out of Shanghai, Chinese authorities heard that two of his men were dead, three captured. Other reports were confusing. One listed two more as drowned while trying to escape up a river. Another had them committing suicide to evade arrest.

When Doolittle arrived in Chuchow, he insisted upon seeing the military governor. At the headquarters of General Ko Cho-tung, commanding the Third Military Zone, at Shang-jao, the colonel and Hilger underscored the importance of freeing the captured crews and of sending out search parties for fliers who still might be hiding from the enemy.

Immediately, Chinese guerillas began exploring the seacoast southward from Hangchow Bay. All sampans and junks were alerted to look for Americans who might have crashed in the sea. Before Doolittle and Hilger left headquarters, General Ko hosted a sumptuous banquet. The Americans were surprised to find the best French wines adorning the table and, after dinner, savored excellent cognac with their hosts.

Doolittle was deeply troubled about Farrow and Hallmark. He pleaded with the Chinese military to launch an offensive against the area where it was reported the Americans were imprisoned. The generals protested. Their forces were too weak, their weapons too impotent to engage the Japanese.

The colonel then urged negotiations and ransom. "Pay them anything they ask," Doolittle told the Chinese, "Don't haggle over the price."

It was 1900 hours, 25 April, when Hallmark, Meder, and Nielsen arrived in Tokyo and were transported to Military Police headquarters. Since their capture, they had not shaved, washed, or changed clothes.

The aviators were thrown into solitary confinement and, 15 minutes later, hauled out into a fresh nightmare. Guards tied their hands behind the chairs, their feet to the rungs. Fists smashed their heads and bodies.

From 1930 hours until 0400 hours their guards kept

asking over and over where they'd come from, if they'd bombed Tokyo, if they'd been stationed in China, if they were American Army personnel. From 1930 hours until 0400 hours the fliers resisted.

Lieutenant Farrow's crew, also incarcerated in Tokyo, encountered similar treatment. Gradually, Corporal De-Shazer realized the enemy already knew the details of the raid, the number of planes, the names of the crews, the name of the commander, the take-off from the *Hornet*. Some thoughtless pilot, DeShazer reasoned, had failed to destroy the necessary papers in his plane.

Lieutenant George Barr, standing six feet two and with a blotch of red hair, had become the curiosity at Military Police headquarters. Soldiers came up to his cell and stared again and again. They asked what he ate and drank to get the red hair. Barr told them he'd jumped from a plane and, when he hit the ground, he had landed on his head. He could remember nothing.

Near a village in Kiangsu Province, Bishop Charles Quinn, eight American Roman Catholic priests, five nuns, and 300 Chinese were retreating into the hills to avoid capture by advancing Japanese troops, which swarmed into the area searching for natives who had helped the fliers. Father Humbert Verdini, an Italian Vincentian priest, had volunteered to remain behind to protect the old, the young, the sick. When runners reported to Bishop Quinn the enemy had moved on, the refugees trekked back. Horror-struck, quivering with rage, they surveyed total destruction and desolation. The countryside reeked of death. Their friends lay slaughtered in bloody heaps. Peasants who had stayed on hoping to continue working their fields lay beheaded, their bodies savagely tortured. The Japanese had expended

159

their fury against Chinese who had sheltered the stranded aviators and helped them to escape.

In Chungking, Generalissimo Chiang Kai-shek filed a cablegram to the United States government. Entire populations of the coastal areas had been wiped out. The brutality of the Nazi leveling of the Czech village of Lidice, lamented the Generalissimo, had been reproduced on a grand scale in eastern China.

A Japanese expeditionary force of 100,000 men had begun a campaign of terror to discourage the Chinese from further collaboration. Infuriated by the Tokyo raid, intoxicated by the taste of triumph, the Japanese wasted and ravaged the land. In three months they drove their bayonets 200 miles through the heart of East China, destroying, plowing up fields, exterminating every individual remotely suspected. Entire villages, through which the aviators had drifted, were slaughtered to the last child and burned to the ground. One sizeable city was flattened for no other reason than the sentiment displayed by its citizens in filling up Japanese bomb craters. More than 600 enemy air raids preceded the advancing army. The Japanese were to kill 250,000 Chinese soldiers and civilians in this three-month campaign of devastation. The Chinese people paid dearly for the Tokyo raid.

Ted Lawson spent a bad night in Linhai. He was toxic from his wounds and the sulfa. More effective treatment was indicated. Since Griff Williams and Lawson were both Type A, Doc White gambled on a direct transfusion with two ancient syringes, the only apparatus available. Experiencing difficulty with clogged needles and syringes, White managed to run in 150cc of blood on the first try and, on the second, 200cc. Lawson noticeably improved. White saw no reason to keep Don Smith, Williams, Sessler, Saylor, and Thatcher around town. He ordered them to Chuchow. When Thatcher said goodbye to his pilot, it was doubtful whether Lawson would pull through.

A week later, White decided to amputate. With novocain the Chinese had smuggled out of Shanghai, Lawson was given a spinal anesthetic. One of the missionaries who was a trained nurse, sterilized the packs and antiquated instruments, then scrubbed with White and Dr. Chen.

They had exhausted the anesthetic when the operation ended. Lawson recalled he felt only the last few stitches. After the ordeal, White gave Lawson another 500cc of blood. Lacking an A-type donor, White gave the blood, himself, as he was Type O, a "universal donor."

The following day, 5 May, Lawson was better. For the first time since the crash, he was comfortable, more lucid. By this time, Davenport and Clever were up and about, hobbling on crutches or canes, and McClure was walking, although his shoulders still pained.

By mid-May, the Japanese forces were moving up fast toward Linhai. Army headquarters had pulled out. There were not enough soldiers and artillery to defend the city. One month after the Tokyo strike, the Americans hurried preparations for escaping. After a substantial breakfast, they were packed into sedan chairs and started off. Dr. Chen acted as an interpreter. There was an armed escort, and coolies lugged the baggage. Crossing and recrossing the river, sometimes on bridges, more often on ferries, the party moved through the countryside.

The town of Lishui rang with the clanging and cursing of military confusion as White, Lawson, and the others rode in. They glimpsed companies of troops

161

marching off for battle equipped with Chinese rifles, Bren guns, potato-masher grenades, but no heavy stuff. Against this force, the Japanese were throwing airplanes, tanks, and artillery.

A 1941 station wagon rumbled down the narrow streets. The Americans scrambled in except for Lawson, who was loaded into a truck. These were the last two vehicles to leave Lishui.

In the station wagon the fliers luxuriated in easing back into the leather cushions as they bounded and bounced up the road at a clip 50 times faster than that of sedan chairs.

At every bridge the Americans saw refugees waiting silently. As soon as the station wagon and truck rolled by, there was a dull boom as the bridge was demolished. After they had rattled over a straight stretch of road, coolies closed in behind, laboring feverishly to destroy the highway. Abandoning the station wagon and truck, the party continued by bus and train to safety.

At a Canadian mission station in the village of Yang Kou, American Methodist missionary John Birch talked with Reverend C. T. Paulson. Colonel Doolittle had made available 2000 dollars, Chinese, and the Canadian requested Birch to purchase a grave near Chuchow and to bury Corporal Leland Faktor, who had perished in the jump.

That night John Birch took the train for Chuchow where, several days later, he held memorial services for Corporal Faktor. Major Y. C. Chen, representing the Chinese Air Force, presented the United States Army Air Corps with a free burial plot. At the grave near the main group of buildings at army headquarters, Birch committed Faktor on 19 May with full military honors.

162

In Tokyo's Military Police headquarters, eight Americans languished in prisons while high-ranking Japanese authorities argued whether to treat them as prisoners of war or war criminals. General Sugiyama, Chief of the Japanese General Staff, insisted that those who had bombed Tokyo were war criminals and demanded their prompt execution.

Premier Tojo questioned Sugiyama's harshness. Japan, he countered, had no law authorizing the death penalty to captured airmen. Then he ordered authorities to draw up a statute imposing the death penalty so Japan could apply it, if need be, to the aviators. With such a law, Tojo planned to deter other aviators. This conflict between the Chief of Staff and the Premier delayed the trial.

Meanwhile the jailers continued questioning and buffeting the prisoners. "What are the designated airfields in China?" "Where is the extra gasoline stored?" The interrogators showed them maps salvaged from the downed planes.

Under incessant questioning and torture, the Americans confessed to the bombing of Tokyo, discussed the target areas and the carrier take-offs. Other than the bare outline of the raid, the men said little beyond giving routine biographical information.

On the basis of these answers, the inquisitors drew up papers—"It was like a book," declared Barr—all in Japanese for the aviators to sign. To reassure them, the guards read relatively innocuous statements in English. The planes had hit steel mills, factories, and other military installations. The Japanese did not indicate to the fliers that the indictments contained their "confessions" to bombing schools, shrines, and hospitals. Tricked, under

163

duress, the Yanks signed the indictments written in incomprehensible Japanese.

Bill Farrow's signature appeared on a document, which included the following.

"Didn't you actually bomb innocent civilians?"

"I don't know what excuse to make for that other than to state the fact, we were a temporary crew with inadequate training. I cannot make any assertion that we bombed our targets and nothing else. Moreover, at that time the Japanese antiaircraft guns were very active, and since our only thought was to drop our bombs quickly and make a hurried dash for safety, I believe it is natural that some damage was inflicted on residences, and some civilians may have been killed. On this score, as commander of the plane, I am fully cognizant of my responsibilities."

"Wasn't that point made clear in Colonel Doolittle's order?"

"No. We saw the decisions regarding the selection of the primary objective of the air raid was really to demoralize the Japanese people; it was natural, as far as we were concerned, that bombings of innocent civilians would be one of the methods. Also, since our pre-designated objective, Osaka, was unexpectedly changed to Nagoya, I could only guess at the location of our target."

"While heading out to sea from Nagoya, didn't you strafe children at school?"

"There is truly no excuse for this. I have made no mention of this incident before, but after leaving Nagoya, I do not quite remember the place, there was a place which looked like a school, with many people there. As a parting shot, with a feeling of 'damn these Japs,' I made a power dive and carried out some strafing. There was absolutely no defensive fire from below."

Bob Meder, co-pilot with Hallmark, looked at the undecipherable pigeon tracks and was duped into signing a "confession," which included:

"You not only bombed factories, but you also bombed homes of the innocent. What are your reactions?"

"It is natural that dropping bombs on a crowded place like Tokyo will cause damage in the vicinity of the target. All the more so with our technique, of dropping our bombs while making a hit-and-run attack, so I believe it was unavoidable. Also, Doolittle never did order us to avoid such bombings and neither were we particularly worried about the possible damages."

"Don't you feel sorry for the innocent women and children?"

"Personally, I am extremely sorry, but in modern warfare such things cannot be helped. Inasmuch as demoralizing the spirit of the people is one of the objectives, there is no alternative other than to ignore our feelings."

The other six Americans signed similar statements. The Japanese used these captives as whipping boys for the bombing errors of the entire Tokyo mission.

Hallmark and Meder were in wretched shape. Nielsen's leg wounds, caused by the continuous beatings, were infected. So were the louse bites on all the fliers. They received no medical treatment and were denied baths, shaves, and fresh clothing.

The fortunate began arriving in Chungking. In a ramshackle house on a hillside, Colonel Doolittle, dressed in a torn, muddy, wool shirt and trousers, with no mark of rank on his shoulders, sat astride a broken chair and told his story to air intelligence officers. "I don't know," he said, "whether I'm due for general court-martial or a slap on the back, for we bombed Tokyo all right; we bombed the hell out of it, by God, we did, but I think I'm the only commanding officer of an air outfit in history who ever lost all his airplanes—lost all of them, lost every damned one—yet accomplished his mission, and maybe made a good job of it."

Colonel Clayton Bissell, Stilwell's air officer, greeted Doolittle. "Hap cabled me to let me know he'd signed your commission as a Brigadier General." All the aviators received Distinguished Flying Crosses and, later, as a result of the mission, Doolittle was awarded the Congressional Medal of Honor.

The wounded were sent to stateside hospitals. The others were reassigned, a handful returning home to participate in bond rallies and patriotic gatherings. During the next 12 months, the luck of several raiders ran out. Lieutenant Eugene McGurl and Sergeants Melvin J. Gardner and Omer A. Duquette failed to return from missions; Lieutenant Robert Gray perished in the Asiatic Theater; Lieutenants Kenneth Reddy and Robert Clever died in crashes in the states; Lieutenant Richard E. Miller and Sergeant Paul Leonard were killed in action in North Africa; Lieutenant Donald G. Smith met death in the European Theater; Captain David Jones, after distinguished flying in North Africa, became a German prisoner of war.

Before leaving China, Doolittle made arrangements with Madame Chiang Kai-shek to seek to ransom the captured fliers. Guerilla bands were promised huge sums of money for each prisoner brought out alive.

Army headquarters in Tokyo decided to sentence the men to death. Premier Tojo protested. General Sugiyama, Chief of Staff, went directly to Tojo and demanded the death penalty. Backing down under fire, the premier ordered the executions. Discussions followed between Army General Headquarters and Military Police over where the mock trial should be convened. Shanghai was selected.

Manacled, legcuffed, and rope-tied, the prisoners were herded from their Tokyo cells. One airman turned, blind-mad, and screamed, "Sure we bombed your damned town. And we'll bomb it again. We'll bomb it twice and three times. I'll bomb it as often as God will let me." He and the others were led off to the train.

They'd not washed for 60 days. On the first leg of the journey to Shanghai, coal soot from the locomotive filtering into the cars smeared their faces, hair, and uniforms. At Nagasaki, guards threw them into prison cells for the night. The Americans, all suffering from dysentery, almost vomited at the stench.

Guarded closely, five other Americans were on board the Trans-Siberian railroad jolting their way toward western Russia in a rickety, third-class passenger coach hooked like a caboose to the rear of a freight train. Lighted at night by candles, their partitionless coach contained double compartments, which opened into an aisle running the entire length of the car. The seats were wooden. The floor was carpetless. The rear end of the car was provisioned with 20 loaves of black bread, three-foot long Bologna sausages, cases of vodka, tea, sugar— their rations during the extended journey.

Except for a shower they wangled at Omsk on the 14th day out from Khabarovsk, the Americans remained padlocked on the train for the entire trip. For miles the Trans-Siberian railroad was single track and, as troop trains had priority, the freight was often shunted to sidings where delays were long. During one 24-hour stretch, the train jerked forward only a half mile.

Everywhere along the way, the airmen saw filth and poverty. At the depots, hundreds of beggars swarmed, dirty fingers upraised, voices crying out for crumbs. Beyond in the stations, York and his crew noticed that every Russian looked destitute. Old and young, shabby in their rags, shuffled about with vacant stares. Even the dogs shuffled. Guards at many of the stations, armed with pistols and billy clubs, turned savagely on the beggars clustered about the passenger coach.

At Omsk, the train puffed to a halt in the morning. Appalled at the squalor outside their car windows, the Americans listened to one of their guards strumming a guitar and droning patriotic songs. The Russian officer, Michael Schmaring—"Mike" to the Americans—their interpreter and escort, arranged for the captives to shower in a primitive shack near the station. All of the train guards went along, always in a protective, flanking position. Going to and from the bath house, the party resembled a drill squad of buck privates.

The locomotive didn't budge from Omsk until nearly midnight. The fliers snacked on black bread and caviar, washing it down with vodka. Just as they refilled the tumblers, a rock smashed through the window and showered glass in all directions. No one was hurt. The Americans surmised that beggars, peering through the cracks in the curtains, had spied them eating.

The train jerked its way from Asiatic Russia into Europe. Travel became faster and steadier. On the 17th day of their trip, Mike casually remarked they'd arrive in Kuibyshev in the morning. This was the city where all foreign embassies had fled during the siege of Moscow.

Would they be permitted to visit the American Embassy? No. Such procedures were dangerous, unwise. Too many Japanese lived and worked in Kuibyshev. Momentarily disheartened, the aviators didn't doubt that embassy representatives would meet the freight. This would give the diplomats a chance to inspect their wretched quarters, the Bologna-type food, the gun-toting guards. Anyway, they reasoned, they were going to see their first Americans since the take-off a month previous. They would learn the fate of the other raiders and might even, possibly, receive mail from home.

That evening, they shined shoes and buttons, freshened their uniforms, and listed the things they lacked— toothpaste, toothbrushes, shaving soap, lotion, cigarettes.

All were up early the next day. The train clattered into Kuibyshev at 0530 hours, hissing to a stop. As Mike clambered off, the fliers pleaded with him to contact the American Embassy just in case they had forgotten about the fliers and the train.

They waited alone in the locked coach. Outside one guard, cradling his tommy gun, stood at the door. Equipped with a similar weapon, the other picket patrolled the station.

The wait stretched out. The Russians in the depot were the most impoverished, the most ravenous, the most sullen-looking crowd the Americans had ever seen.

Noon came and went. No embassy representative appeared. The sentries still paced up and down outside. The airmen tried to jimmy the door to the food locker. Failing, they opened their emergency rations of beef and gravy, which they'd lugged away from their bomber.

At 1600 hours they still waited. Mike stumbled in an hour later, stinking of vodka, his face flushed from the Turkish bath he'd recently taken. Had he contacted the embassy? No. Why would he? To the Yanks it became obvious the Soviets had not informed the embassy of their arrival. While they ate dinner that night, the train pulled

169

out of the station, going west, away from the legation.

The next day, section hands unshackled the passenger coach, which rolled to a stop on a siding. There was no depot, but four automobiles were parked along the tracks. When the Americans jumped to the ground, accompanied by the guards, six Russian officers greeted them warmly and welcomed them to Okhuna, a village seven miles from the city of Penza. The autos started up and barreled off down the rutted road. Before reaching Okhuna, the cars veered right and sped along a road bordered on one side by a high fence. After a grinding halt at the gate, they entered the grounds. Mike ushered the birdmen into their living quarters. York took a room alone, while Herndon and Emmens shared another and the two enlisted men, Laban and Pohl, occupied a third. They all agreed the rooms were comfortable. Each was furnished with a bed, huge table, leather chair, potted fern, mirror, and washstand. In the center of the building there was a make-shift room for the guards.

Pulling out a map, Mike fingered the village of Okhuna, then located Penza and Moscow. They were 300 miles to the south and east of the capital, west of the Volga River.

The Americans eased into the daily routine. At 0930 hours was breakfast; at 1330 hours, dinner; at 1800 hours, tea and sweet rolls; at 2100 hours, supper. The meals of fresh meat and vegetables were far superior to the bread and Bologna diet of the train. During the day, they chatted with the women servants and guards, picking up Russian words, playing endless games of chess. In the evenings, they fiddled with the radio and listened to the news from Moscow. Occasionally, the dull regimen was broken when the Russians showed full-length motion pictures complete with sound. The airmen saw the four-hour version of "Peter the Great" at one sitting, the normal length "Suborov," and one American movie, "One Hundred Men and a Girl." Through the movies, the news broadcast, the chess games, the men's minds concentrated on one question. When would the embassy contact them?

One morning, three autos entered the gates. In the first sat Colonel Joseph Michella, American military attaché to the Soviet Union, and Mr. Page, a secretary in the embassy. The other cars were loaded with Russian officers. After a tour of the grounds, Michella insisted that he and Page meet alone with the five aviators.

York and his crew blurted out their experiences from the time of the launch until they reached Okhuna. When they reported their layover in Kuibyshev, Michella explained that the embassy knew of their trip from eastern Russia, but had no idea that they were in the city until after they had departed.

Frankly, the colonel told the fliers, getting internees out of Russia wasn't easy. The Soviets were deeply troubled about the chance of a war in the Far East. If the Americans were released and sent home, they feared hostilities with Japan. It was too risky. Michella assured the fliers, however, that the embassy was already drawing up a plan for their freedom.

The colonel then turned to Emmens and asked if he'd been given any messages. On learning he had not, Michella handed the lieutenant a telegram in Russian, which Page quickly translated. Emmens was the proud father of a redheaded son, born 18 May. Mother and baby doing fine. After much whooping and backslapping, they asked about the other raiders. Michella wasn't sure. The States had clamped strict security on the entire operation. There was little news at the embassy.

The colonel presented the airmen with two cardboard

cartons crammed with soap, shirts, socks, cigarettes, and seven magazines, two *Colliers'*, three *Saturday Evening Posts*, two *Lifes*. Out on the veranda, the Americans rejoined the patiently waiting Russians. After lunch and a toast to final victory, the embassy officials and the military were off.

Gloomily, the internees returned to tedium. York thought they would be in Russia for at least another month. They stayed over a year. After being shunted from one town to another, they finally escaped into Iran.

Clamped into Shanghai's infamous Bridge House on 19 June 1942, eight aviators surveyed their 12-foot by 15-foot cell. Fifteen others—Chinese, Japanese, Jews, Dutch, French—mingled, elbowed, jabbered. A symphonic stink eddied about the cell. It was the stink of human smells, of urine and excrement, of vomit and sickness, of sweat and filth. Every day of the 70 they were confined at Bridge House, each received a pint of conji (watery rice) for breakfast, four ounces of bread for lunch, four ounces of bread for supper. Among themselves they split two quarts of water a day.

The weather turned hot. Hallmark was so sick he was on a stretcher continually. There was not enough room for all 23 to lie down at the same time. At night they took turns and flopped on the wooden floor. Diabolically, the guards startled the prisoners from sound sleep, forcing them to stand, threatening them with clubs which they poked through the bars. During the day, they ordered the aviators to sit straight up on the floor without support for their backs. One day, a jailer caught Hite and Farrow leaning against the wall. Bellowing *Kurah* (Hey!), he swung open the cell door and hit them on their heads with his steel scabbard. Hite, in a fit of anger, grabbed at the weapon. The Japanese pulled the sword from the scabbard, raised it, aimed it at Hite's head, hesitated, then strode from the cell.

Days lengthened into weeks. Hallmark, plagued with severe dysentery, passed out one morning and, after that, he worsened. His comrades began regular shifts around the clock, carrying him to the latrine every 15 minutes, but this schedule soon became too arduous for them. They were still subjected to periodic interrogation.

On 28 August, the Americans were taken to the Civic Assembly Area for trial. Hallmark lay on his stretcher. The court-martial was headed by a prosecutor and three judges. From Tokyo, Colonel Arisue had already arrived bringing personal word from General Sugiyama. He expected the death penalty for each flier.

For the aviators, there was no defense counsel, no witnesses, no charges, no interpreters, no chance to plead. After each of the eight prisoners recited his name, rank, serial number, and sketched his education and Air Corps training, a judge stood up and read a manuscript in Japanese. This cited evidence of the indiscriminate bombing of Tokyo in which innocent people were killed. Such attacks, the report went on, were against military law. The court, therefore, was instructed to hand down the death penalty.

Furiously, Nielsen demanded an interpreter. His request was denied. Barr was so weak he began to totter until guards brought in a chair. Hallmark was unconscious most of the time, and his friends doubted if he knew what was going on.

The farcical trial lasted twenty minutes. Speaking in Japanese, the judges condemned the eight men to death. The Americans were not informed. The guards transported Hallmark back to Bridge House, but escorted the others to solitary confinement cells at Kiangwan prison.

At the new prison, each flier was caged in a nine-by-five-foot cell with a grass mat and three blankets. Lice and fleas thrived. Three times a day they bolted down rice and soup and, occasionally, fish. They still wore their filthy uniforms, although there at Kiangwan, they bathed once a week. Most of the time, except for a half hour of exercising a day, they sat and stared at the four walls. If they stood up and tried to stretch or walk around, the jailer ran down the corridor and forced them to sit down and be quiet. The fearful anxiety continued.

In Tokyo, jealousies and rivalries between the army and cabinet flared. On 3 October, both Premier Tojo and General Sugiyama had audiences with Emperor Hirohito. Tojo arrived first at the Imperial Palace, reported the details of the capture, trial, and proposed sentence, and advocated a lighter punishment. This report was received by the Emperor, the only authority who could reduce the sentences. Tojo trusted the humane nature of the Emperor—he would want to execute the smallest number of prisoners.

Later that afternoon, General Sugiyama went to the Palace, formally demanded death, and urged that such executions be carried out with dispatch. Had the general talked with the Emperor prior to Tojo's arrival, all prisoners would probably have been shot. But the premier had reached the Palace first. The Emperor reprieved five of the eight Americans. Only those who had "confessed" to killing school children were scheduled for the firing squad.

On 10 October, Sugiyama wired General Shunroku Hata, commanding officer in occupied China:

The verdict issued by the military tribunal concerning the punishment of the American airmen is considered to be fair and just. However, upon review, we believe that with the exception of both pilots and gunner Spatz, the death sentence should be commuted. On the 13th of this month, Lt. Col. Takayama will depart from Fukuoka in connection with the case, and shall appreciate it if you will keep him informed as to the execution of the sentence.

Another telegram was sent to General Hata:

Sentence to death, Hallmark, Farrow, Spatz. (2) Death sentence commuted, Meder, Nielsen, Hite, Barr, DeShazer. Time of execution about 15 October. The five whose death sentences were commuted shall be sentenced to life. As war criminals, their treatment shall not be that accorded ordinary prisoners of war. Even in the event of an exchange of war prisoners they may not be repatriated to the United States.

Alexander Hindrava, a Soviet broker in Shanghai, was arrested and locked up in cell no. 6, Bridge House. After adjusting his eyes to the dim light, he noticed a crumpled figure lying on the floor in a blanket—a bearded, starving skeleton, suffering from chronic dysentery, his bowels moving by themselves every few minutes. This tortured creature was Dean Hallmark. Half delirious, he mumbled that he did not know why he was there. He was an American pilot who had bombed military installations in a Japanese city and should be in a prisoner of war camp, not a civilian jail. His words trailed off in a gibberish sound.

Every few minutes, Hindrava helped the pilot to the wooden bucket in the corner.

The cell door clanked open. Too weak to walk by himself, Hallmark stumbled a few steps, then collapsed. Hindrava supported him out of the cell, where a Japanese corporal took him down the corridor. Hallmark smiled and murmured that finally he was going to a prisoner-of-war camp, where he'd receive proper food and parcels from home.

At 1610 hours, 15 October, outside of Shanghai, a black limousine halted in the bleak First Cemetery grounds. Hallmark, Farrow, and Spatz, handcuffed and surrounded by soldiers, stepped out. Off in the distance stood a group of officers.

Captain Sotojiro Tatsuta asked the prisoners for any last words. Warrant Officer Shigeji Mayama, the prison gravedigger, saw the prisoners lean over and whisper a few sentences which he could not understand. Prison guards marched the Americans to three crosses, tied them with fresh cloth, draped white hoods over their heads, marking black X's on them just above their noses.

Upon command, the six-man squad fired. Hallmark, Farrow, and Spatz slumped. An Army medical officer walked forward and examined the bodies. Warrant Officer Mayama then assisted in placing the airmen into separate coffins.

Two days later, the other five airmen were dragged into court. Standing before the judge, they looked around for Hallmark, Farrow, and Spatz. From the way the judge was reading the long statement in Japanese, they calculated that this was the death sentence. All five were to face the firing squad for killing innocent Japanese; but, said the interpreter, by the gracious consent of the Emperor, their sentences had been commuted to life. They were marched back to their cells, destined to spend all but 70 days of the next 40 months in solitary confinement.

That night, Bob Meder carved on the wooden floor, "Lieut. R. J. Meder, USAF, 0-421280, B-25 Bomber Command Detail plane No. 2298. Please notify U. S. Army life imprisonment." It was his epitaph.

Bob Meder died in December 1944 in solitary confinement. Barr, Hite, DeShazer, and Nielsen were rescued from Peiping by an American parachute team on 20 August 1945.

EPILOGUE

At 2313 hours, Eastern wartime, 20 May 1942, General James H. Doolittle was finishing his radio talk to the nation. "The greatest result of our raid," he remarked, "is the material and psychological damage we inflicted upon the enemy. In neither respect is the enemy likely to recover soon."

Doolittle continued, "My faith in the American fighting men in American planes has never been so strong. We have in our training centers, on our production lines, the pattern from which will be built many more surprises for Japan and Germany. It is the ultimate pattern for our own victory."

The Tokyo Raid proved the need for the long-contemplated Japanese invasion against Midway Island and the western Aleutians. Japanese strategists believed that by occupying Midway and establishing bases in the Aleutians, they could preclude another carrier strike against the homeland. Significantly, the raid forced the Japanese to analyze Tokyo's defenses and to station four army pursuit groups in the home islands during 1942–43, when fighters were desperately sought for the Solomons campaign.

The Tokyo Raid marked both an end and a beginning for the Americans. It ended five lean months of unmitigated bad news. The mission marked, by happy co-incidence, the start of the Allied drive in the Far East. Although New Guinea and the Aleutians would yield the enemy limited, temporary successes, there would be no more big victories except for the fall of already-doomed Corregidor. After the Tokyo attack, came the Coral Sea victory, then Midway, then the landings on Guadalcanal. The Eighteenth of April, like a false dawn, held the promise of eventual victory in the Pacific.

APPENDIX

THE COMBAT CREWS

AIRPLANE #1

Pilot	Lt. Col. J. H. Doolittle
Co-pilot	Lt. R. E. Cole
Navigator	Lt. H. A. Potter
Bombardier	S/Sgt. F. A. Braemer
Engineer Gunner	S/Sgt. P. J. Leonard

AIRPLANE #2

Pilot	Lt. Travis Hoover
Co-pilot	Lt. Wm. N. Fitzhugh
Navigator	Lt. Carl R. Wildner
Bombardier	Lt. Richard E. Miller
Engineer Gunner	S/Sgt. Douglas V. Radney

AIRPLANE #3

Pilot	Lt. Robert M. Gray
Co-pilot	Lt. Jacob E. Manch
Navigator Gunner	Lt. Chas. J. Ozuk
Bombardier	Sgt. A. E. Jones
Engineer Gunner	Cpl. Leland D. Faktor

AIRPLANE #4

Pilot	Lt. Everett W. Holstrom
Co-pilot	Lt. Lucian N. Youngblood
Navigator Gunner	Lt. Harry C. McCool
Bombardier	Sgt. Robert J. Stephens
Engineer Gunner	Cpl. Bert M. Jordan

AIRPLANE #5

Pilot	Capt. David M. Jones
Co-pilot	Lt. Rodney R. Wilder
Navigator Gunner	Lt. Eugene F. McGurl
Bombardier	Lt. Denver V. Truelove
Engineer Gunner	Sgt. Joseph W. Manske

AIRPLANE #6

Pilot	Lt. Dean E. Hallmark
Co-pilot	Lt. Robert J. Meder
Navigator Gunner	Lt. Chase J. Nielsen
Bombardier	Sgt. Wm. J. Dieter
Engineer Gunner	Cpl. Donald E. Fitzmaurice

AIRPLANE #7

Pilot	Lt. Ted W. Lawson
Co-pilot	Lt. Dean Davenport
Navigator Gunner	Lt. Chas. L. McClure
Bombardier	Lt. Robt. S. Clever
Engineer Gunner	Sgt. David J. Thatcher

AIRPLANE #8

Pilot	Capt. Edward J. York
Co-pilot	Lt. Robert G. Emmens
Navigator Bombardier	Lt. Nolan A. Herndon
Engineer Gunner	S/Sgt. T. H. Laban
Gunner	Sgt. David W. Pohl

AIRPLANE #9

Pilot	Lt. Harold F. Watson
Co-pilot	Lt. James M. Parker, Jr.
Navigator Gunner	Lt. Thos. C. Griffin
Bombardier	Sgt. Wayne M. Bissell
Engineer Gunner	T/Sgt. Eldred V. Scott

AIRPLANE #10

Pilot	Lt. Richard O. Joyce
Co-pilot	Lt. J. Royden Stork
Navigator Bombardier	Lt. H. E. Crouch
Engineer Gunner	Sgt. Geo. E. Larkin, Jr.
Gunner	S/Sgt. Ed. W. Horton, Jr.

AIRPLANE #11

Pilot	Capt. Chas. R. Greening
Co-pilot	Lt. Kenneth E. Reddy
Navigator Gunner	Lt. Frank A. Kappeler
Bombardier	S/Sgt. Wm. L. Birch
Engineer Gunner	Sgt. Melvin J. Gardner

AIRPLANE #12

Pilot	Lt. Wm. M. Bower
Co-pilot	Lt. Thadd Blanton
Navigator Gunner	Lt. Wm. R. Pound, Jr.
Bombardier	T/Sgt. Waldo J. Bither
Engineer Gunner	S/Sgt. Omer A. Duquette

AIRPLANE #13

Pilot	Lt. Edgar E. McElroy
Co-pilot	Lt. Richard A. Knobloch
Navigator Gunner	Lt. Clayton J. Campbell
Bombardier	Sgt. Robert C. Bourgeois
Engineer Gunner	Sgt. Adam R. Williams

AIRPLANE #14

Pilot	Major John A. Hilger
Co-pilot	Lt. Jack A. Sims
Navigator Bombardier	Lt. James H. Macia, Jr.
Engineer Gunner	S/Sgt. Jacob Eierman
Radio Gunner	S/Sgt. Edwin V. Bain

AIRPLANE #15

Pilot	Lt. Donald G. Smith
Co-pilot	Lt. Griffith P. Williams
Navigator Bombardier	Lt. Howard A. Sessler
Flight Surgeon	Lt. Thomas R. White, (M.D.)
Engineer Gunner	Sgt. Edward J. Saylor

AIRPLANE #16

Pilot	Lt. Wm. G. Farrow
Co-pilot	Lt. Robert L. Hite
Navigator Gunner	Lt. Geo. Barr
Bombardier	Cpl. Jacob DeShazer
Engineer Gunner	Sgt. Harold A. Spatz

BIBLIOGRAPHY

Manuscripts. National Archives: "B25B Special Project. Plans;" Betts, T. J., to Asst. Chief of Staff, G-2, 20 April 1942; Cooper, Col. Merian, "The Doolittle Air Raid on Japan Known as First Aviation Project." Report; "Doolittle, Brig. Gen. James H., "Report of the Aerial Bombing of Japan, 5 June 1942;" International Military Tribunal, Far East, "Proceedings," "Transcripts;" Johnson, Maj. Harvey, "Report;" Logbooks of the *Hornet, Enterprise, Trout, Thresher, Cimarron, Nashville;* McGhee, Capt. J., "Report of Interviews with Lt. H. C. McCool and Sergeant W. J. Bither, 23 August 1942;" Patterson, Col. Earl S., to Julius Amberg (Special Asst. to Sec. of War regarding Senate Investigation) n.d.;" Pinkney, Maj. J. F., "The Memoranda of Personal Interviews;" Spencer, Robert S. to Col. Bicknell, 22 May 1942; White, Lt. Thomas Robert, "Report to Air Surgeon, 23 June 1942." Navy Department, Office of Naval History, Classified Operational Archives: CINCPAC Report, 4 May 1942; Correspondence relating to Medals Returned to Tokyo; Mitscher, M. A., Commanding Officer, Report of Action, to Commander in Chief U.S. Pacific Fleet, 28 April 1942; Narratives from Captain C. W. Fox, SC, USN, Lt. Robin M. Lindsey, USN, Commander E. B. Mott, USN, Captain Frederick L. Riefkohl, USN, Lt. John F. Sutherland, USN; War Diaries of *Cimarron, Nashville,* CINCPAC, *Thresher, Trout, Enterprise, Hornet,*

Squadron VB-3, *Meredith.* Library of Congress, Manuscript Division: General H. H. Arnold Papers. Department of the Army, Chief of Military History: Marshall, S.L.A. "Tokyo Raid." Air University, Maxwell Air Force Base: Miller, Lt. Henry L., "Official Report, 7 May 1942." Hoover Institution on War, Revolution, and Peace, Stanford University, Calif.: General Joseph W. Stilwell Papers.

Printed Sources. Newspapers: *New York Times, New York Herald Tribune, Washington Post, San Francisco Chronicle, Los Angeles Times. Asahi Shimbun. Domei Jumpo* (10 day periodical), *Japanese Times & Advertiser, Osaka Mainichi.* Books, articles, reports: (* denotes written by one of the raiders) Arnold, H. H., *Global Mission* (Harper, 1949); *Blanton, Thadd, "Report of Tokyo Raid," *Confidential AAFSAT Intelligence Reports* (1943); Chennault, Claire, *Way of a Fighter,* ed. by Robert Hotz (Putnam, 1949); *Christian Century,* 29 April 1942, 5 May 1943; Craven, Wesley Frank, *et al, The Army Air Forces in World War II* (Univ. of Chicago, 1948) , vol. 1; *Eierman, Jacob, "I Helped Bomb Japan," *Popular Science* (1943) ; *Emmens, Lt. Col. Robert G., *Guests of the Kremlin* (Macmillan, 1949); Field, John, "Tokyo Raid," *Life,* 3 May 1943; Ford, M. C., "Slow Death in a Japanese Cage," *Colliers'* (1942) ; Grew, Joseph C., *Ten Years in Japan* (Simon and Schuster, 1944) ; Griffin, Alexander A., *A Ship to Remember* (Howell, Soskin, 1943); Halsey, Fleet Admiral William F., & Lt. Comdr. J. Bryan III, *Admiral Halsey's Story* (Whittlesey House, 1947) ; "Japanese Air Tactics—Pilots," *Informational Intelligence Summary No. 52;* *Hilger, Col. John, "Tokyo Raid," *Life,* 3 May 1943; King, Admiral Ernest J. & Walter Muir Whitehill, *Fleet Admiral King* (Norton, 1952) ; *Lawson, Ted W., *Thirty Seconds over Tokyo,* ed. by Robert Considine (Random House, 1943) ; Morris, John, *Traveler from Tokyo* (Sheridan House, 1944); Morison, Samuel Eliot, *History of United States Naval Operations in World War II* (Little Brown, 1955), vol. III; *Newsweek,* 1 June 1942, 26 April, 3 May 1943; Reynolds, Quentin J., *The Amazing Mr. Doolittle* (Appleton Century, 1953) ; *Shuppan Keisatsu Hô,* 1942–43; *Sims, Col. Jack A., "Tokyo Raid—An Avenging Call," *Air Power Historian* (1957); *Time,* 27 April, 17 June 1942, 3 May 1943; "The Tokyo Raid, April 18, 1942: Objectives, Preparation, The Action,

Enemy Resistance, Mechanical Equipment, Conclusions," *Informational Intelligence Summary Special No. 20;* Tolischus, Otto D., *Tokyo Record* (Reynal, 1943) ; United States Army Air Forces, *Mission Accomplished; Interrogations of Japanese Industrial, Military and Civil Leaders of World War II* (1946) ; United States Office of Strategic Services, Research and Analysis Branch, *Information Gathered on S.S. Gripsholm* (1942); United States Strategic Bombing Survey, *The Effects of Strategic Bombing on Japanese Morale* (1947); Watson, Charles Hoyt, *The Amazing Story of Sergeant Jacob DeShazer* (Light and Life Press, 1950) ; *White, Maj. Thomas Robert, "The Hornet Stings Japan," *Atlantic Monthly* (1943) . *Personal Interviews.* Army and Navy personnel and Japanese civilians.

NOTES AND REFERENCES

REHEARSAL

13–24   Material for the three opening sections comes from the war diaries of the *Thresher* and *Trout;* the unpublished, manuscript diary of Colonel Paul Bunker, U.S. Army; and interviews. The scene on board the *Vixen* is described in Quentin J. Reynolds', *The Amazing Mr. Doolittle* (1953). The manuscript copy of Captain Donald W. Duncan's preliminary plans are in the National Archives. The discussions between General Henry H. Arnold and Admiral Ernest J. King come from King's, and Walter Muir Whitehill's *Fleet Admiral King* (1952) and Arnold's *Global Mission* (1949). The quote of the boatswain's mate is in Alexander A. Griffin's *A Ship to Remember: The Saga of the Hornet* (1943).

The conversation between Arnold and Doolittle is from the unpublished manuscript report, "The Doolittle Air Raid on Japan Known as the First Special Aviation Project," compiled and written by Colonel Merian C. Cooper. Located in the National Archives, this is the best single source for the Halsey-Doolittle Raid, containing action reports of airmen made at Chungking. The conversation between Hilger and Greening is in Reynolds' *Doolittle,* while the remarks about the selection of the airmen who volunteered is based on the unpublished manuscript history of the raid *Tokyo Raid* by S. L. A. Marshall, a source which was essential to the writing of this book. Ted W. Lawson's *Thirty Seconds over Tokyo* (1943), edited by Robert Considine, is the basis for the quotations by the airmen in Minneapolis. For the description of the modification of the B-25, the author relied almost exclusively on Doolittle's lengthy official report, another excellent source for the Halsey-Doolittle Raid.

25–38   The quotations of the aviators while in the operations shack are from Reynolds' *Doolittle* and Lawson's *Thirty Seconds over Tokyo*. Material relating to the practice take-offs comes from many sources: the unpublished manuscript reports of Lt. Henry L. Miller, USN; Major Harvey Johnson; Doolittle; Cooper; Lt. H. A. Sessler's "Report on the Method Used for Low Altitude Bombing;" statements in the *New York Times,* 21 April 1943; interviews. A pilot's question and Doolittle's answer is contained in Reynolds' *Doolittle.*

The scene at Pearl Harbor and the conversation between Admirals Nimitz and Halsey come from Admiral William H. Halsey's and Lt. Comdr. J. Bryan III's *Admiral Halsey's Story* (1947). Information relating to bombing practice and to the activities of Dr. Thomas R. White is included in Marshall's history, the reports of Cooper and Sessler, the manuscript diary of Dr. White. The meeting in downtown San Francisco between Halsey and Doolittle is described in Reynolds' *Doolittle.* Doolittle's quote while at McClellan Field is in Lawson's *Thirty Seconds over Tokyo.* The aviators' activities at McClellan are described in Cooper's Report. Naval Lieutenant John F. Sutherland's observations are found in his narrative, *Film No. 61.* Corporal Bogart's and Sergeant Royce's actions, including Bogart's quotes, are included in Griffin's *A Ship to Remember.* Reference to an army officer leaving Karachi is in Marshall's history.

39–61   The last night in San Francisco is reconstructed from the files of the *San Francisco Chronicle; Time Magazine,* 3 May 1943; and interviews. The telephone conversation between Marshall and Doolittle is found in Reynolds' *Doolittle*. Mitscher's bull horn instructions to the crew is in Griffin's *A Ship to Remember*. The "Hi-Ho" jingle is in Charles Hoyt Watson's *The Amazing Story of Sergeant Jacob DeShazer* (1950). The quotes relating to the fighting condition of the tanker *Cimarron* comes from her war diary. The description of the training and life on board the *Hornet* is from various sources: "The Tokyo Raid, 18 April 1942: Objectives, Preparation, The Action, Enemy Resistance, Mechanical Equipment, Conclusions," *Informational Intelligence Summary Special No. 20;* Jacob Eierman, "I Helped Bomb Japan," *Popular Science* (1943) ; interviews; Watson's *DeShazer; Time Magazine,* 3 May 1943; the official reports of Cooper, Harvey Johnson, Doolittle; Marshall's history; Navy Correspondence Relating to Medals Returned to Tokyo; Griffin's *A Ship to Remember;* Lawson's *Thirty Seconds over Tokyo;* Reynolds' *Doolittle;* the narratives of naval officers John F. Sutherland *(Film No. 61)*, Robin Lindsey *(Film No. 87D-1)*, C. W. Fox *(Film No. 98)* ; "Japanese Air Tactics—Pilots." *Informational Intelligence Summary No. 52.* Reference to cutting the cards to see which pilot bombed the Imperial Palace is found in Nielsen's testimony in the transcripts of the International Military Tribunal, Far East. Information concerning Chungking is in Marshall's history.

The operations of the *Thresher* and *Trout* are described in their war diaries. The paragraph on pages 52–54 relating to Japanese radio intelligence discovering an enemy task force is from Yoshimori Terai and Kiyoshi Sogawa, former Imperial Japanese Navy commanders, "Homeland Defense Naval Operations, December 1941–March 1943," *Japanese Monograph No. 109,* Part 1. The flight of Alexander and Backus from Chungking is included in Colonel Alexander's official report, which is attached to Cooper's Report. The remarks about the Generalissimo is from Marshall's history. The lengthy quote concerning Reuters is contained in John Field's article in *Life Magazine,* 3 May 1943, and in E. B. Mott's narrative, *Film No. 208.* The description of Tokyo on the eve of the raid is reconstructed from the files of the *Japan Times and Advertiser.*

ATTACK

63–76   Material for the opening paragraphs comes from the war diaries of the *Hornet, Enterprise,* and Squadron VB-3, the narrative of Lt. Robin Lindsey, and Halsey's Action Report. The conversation on board the Japanese patrol vessel comes from *Admiral Halsey's Story.* The *Nashville's* action against the patrol vessel is noted in the cruiser's war diary and Halsey's Action Report. Lt. Sutherland's quote is from his narrative. The bull horn orders for Army personnel to man the planes is from interviews. Reference to the standby crews is in the *Washington Post,* 25 April 1943, while Thadd Blanton's comment is from his article in *Confidential A.A.F.S.A.T. Intelligence Reports* (1943).

The paragraph describing the reactions of the *Enterprises's* crew and the loudspeaker's message is found in Field's article in *Life.* Lt. Manch's actions are described in *Thirty Seconds over Tokyo.* Watson's reactions come from interviews; DeShazer's quote is from Watson's *DeShazer;* the statement concerning George Radulovich is in the *New York Times,* 20 April 1943. Material regarding the fueling of Jones' plane is included in Jones' official report. Hilger's quote is from Eierman's article in *Popular Science.* Chief Engineer Creehan's actions are described in Griffin's *A Ship to Remember.* The conversation between Doolittle and Leonard over the intercom is in Reynolds' *Doolittle.* The naval aviator's quote is from Field's article in *Life.* The account of Doolittle's take-off is in Griffin's *A Ship to Remember.*

Hoover's take-off is reported by Lt. Sutherland in his narrative and by the *New York Times,* 21 April 1943. Data concerning Lawson's take-off is from an interview; York's, from Lt. Col. Robert G. Emmens, *Guests of the Kremlin* (1949); Don Smith's, from his official report. The misfortunes of Bill Farrow's plane are detailed by DeShazer in Watson's *DeShazer.*

The scene in Tokyo just before the raid is based on Marshall's history. Bert Jordan's trouble with the machine gun is described in his official report. The activity described in York's plane is from Emmens' *Guests of the Kremlin.* The account of Watson's bomber is based on material gathered from an interview, and that of Farrow's bomber, from Watson's *DeShazer.*

77–91   The bombing of Tokyo by Doolittle's plane is based on his official report; on the reports of Braemer, Leonard, Potter; on Marshall's history; and also on the remarks of Doolittle and Potter in the *New York Times,* 20 May, 28 June 1942. Reference to the primary school principal is taken from U. S. Strategic Bombing Survey, *The Effects of Strategic Bombing on Japanese Morale* (1947). Doolittle's quote on page 79 is from Reynolds' *Doolittle.* The Japanese private's quote is in Marshall's history.

The reactions of Dr. Kawai is described in U. S. Army Air Force, *Mission Accomplished; Interrogations of Japanese Industrial, Military and Civil Leaders of World War II* (1946). Material concerning P. E. Sato comes from an interview with him in Tokyo. Admiral Shimada's appearance in the Uyeno Fine Arts Museum is reported in the *Japan Times and Advertiser,* 20 April 1942. Information regarding Mr. Oiwa and Mrs. Iwata's quote comes from a personal letter from Florence Wells to the author. The sentence concerning the playing of the "Blue Danube" is taken from the *Japan News and Advertiser,* 18 April 1942.

Data on Hoover's bomb run is contained in the official reports of Hoover, Miller, Wildner; and statements made by Hoover and Miller in an interview with Major J. F. Pinkney. Miller's quote is in his official report; Fitzhugh's comes from the *New York Times,* 25 April 1943.

The paragraph relating to the American offensive is based on Marshall's history. Material on Bob Gray's run across Tokyo comes from the official reports of Gray, Ozuk, Doolittle, and Ozuk's statements in an interview with Major J. F. Pinkney. Ozuk's additional report makes reference to Aden Jones' action with the machine gun.

Information on Holstrom and his plane is in the official reports of Holstrom, McCool, Jordan, Stephens, and Youngblood, and remarks made by McCool in an interview with Captain J. McGhee. The attack made by Sub-Lieutenant Umekawa is described by him in an article in the *Japan Times and Advertiser,* 22 April 1942. For mechanical difficulties, the author also consulted "The Tokyo Raid, 18 April 1942. Objectives, Preparation, The Action, Enemy Resistance, Mechanical Equipment, Conclusions," *Informational Intelligence Summary Special No. 20.*

Jones' attack is described in the official reports of Jones; his and Wilder's statements in an interview with Major Pinkney; Jones' remarks in the *New York Times,* 28 June 1942; and Marshall's history. The action of Hallmark's plane is recreated from Nielsen's testimony in the transcripts of the International Military Tribunal, Far East. The accounts of Lawson's bombing run are in the official reports of Thatcher and Doolittle, statements of Clever and Davenport in interviews with Major Pinkney, Lawson's remarks in the *New York Times,* 23 April 1943, and *Thirty Seconds over Tokyo.* Reference to Lawson's not running along the designated line of objectives comes from Marshall's history.

90–102   The paragraph relating to Joyce and Watson is based on Marshall's history. Material on Watson and his plane, including his thoughts, are from his official report, interviews, Cooper's Report, and from statements of Scott and Parker to Major Pinkney. The run made by Joyce's bomber is reported in the official reports of Joyce and Crouch.

In a personal interview Kikujiro Suzuki of Tokyo describes the Waseda school incident. The remarks of Mrs. Ryu Aoki, Seikichi Honjo, and Katsuzo Yoshida also come from interviews carried on in Tokyo. Reference to an Army hospital being hit is from a censorship report in *Shuppan Keisatsu Hô* and was deleted by Japanese authorities from the Tokyo *Nichi Nichi.* Censors believed that such information would have a bad influence on Japanese morale. The Cabinet decided to prohibit the publication of any statements concerning the damage inflicted. An announcement by Defense General Headquarters on 21 April also indicates that an Army hospital had been destroyed. The remarks of Katsumi Kaneta are in a personal letter to my Japanese research assistant, Taki Kimoto.

The actions of Mrs. Dobashi and Minoru Iida during the raid are described in the *Japan Times and Advertiser,* 20 April 1942. Rev. Bruno Bitter's comments are in U. S. Air Force, *Mission Accomplished; Interrogations of Japanese Industrial, Military and Civil Leaders of World War II.* Reference to John Morris comes from Marshall's history. The Otto Tolischus material is from his book, *Tokyo Record* (1943). Information relating to York's plane, including the quotes, is contained in Emmens' *Guests of the Kremlin.* The scene at the middle school is based on a personal letter from Hiroichi Yamaguchi to my research assistant. The activity at the American Embassy comes from Ambassador Joseph C. Grew's *Ten Years in Japan* (1942), and his statements in the *New York Times,* 1 September 1942. Data on the Argentine Embassy, including the quote by the scrub woman, comes from Ramon Lavalle's remarks in the *New York Times,* 25 April 1943. *The New York Times* of 8 May 1943 carries the statements of Stanislawa Tokalewska. The quote by Eiji Inoui was censored from a magazine article, material which was found in *Shuppan Keisatsu Hô.* The account of the Americans confined in Denenshofu is in Marshall's history.

Accounts of the actions of Greening's plane are in the official reports of Greening, his interview with Major Pinkney, and his statements in the *New York Times,* 21 April 1943. Greening's quote is in the *New York Times,* 28 June 1942. The actions of Miss Florence Wells are detailed in her letter to the author.

Bower's operations are set forth in statements made by him and Pound to Major Pinkney, Bither's remarks to Captain McGhee, and the official reports of Duquette, Bither, Blanton, and Pound. The attack made by McElroy's plane is recounted in the official reports of McElroy, Campbell, Bourgeois, Knobloch.

The attack on Nagoya by Hilger's plane is told in his article in *Life,* 3 May 1943; the official reports of Hilger, Sims, Macia, Bain; Hilger's statements in the *New York Times,* 28 June 1942; Macia's and Sims' remarks to Major Pinkney; Eierman's article in *Popular Science.* The quotes about the baseball game and the guns firing are from Hilger's article in *Life.*

The account of Don Smith's plane is based on the official reports of Smith and Sessler; White's remarks in the *New York Times,* 28 June 1942; statements of White and Smith to Major Pinkney; White's Report to the Air Surgeon; and White's article, "The Hornet Stings Japan," *Atlantic Monthly* (1943). Information which helped reconstruct Farrow's attack comes from DeShazer's remarks in Watson's *DeShazer.*

Captain Riefkohl's statement is in his narrative, *Film No. 331;* and Halsey's, from the unpublished, typewritten copy of "The Navy's Share in the Tokyo Raid." The *Hornet's* war diary and Griffin's *A Ship to Remember* contain Lady Haw Haw's radio talk. The action with the enemy patrol vessels is described in Mitscher's official report; the war diaries of the *Nashville* and Squadron VB-3; the *Enterprise's* war diary and action report; Field's article in *Life.* The jingle about the raid is printed in Griffin's *A Ship to Remember.*

102–108   The 19 April 1942 issue of the *Japan Times and Advertiser* traces the actions of Premier Tojo on the day of the raid. Yuzawa's quote is in the same issue of the *Times;* Shigemitsu's, in the 20 April edition; *Nichi Nichi's* and *Hochi's,* in the 19 April issue. The statement from *Chijinyu* is from a censored, unpublished article found in *Shuppan Keisatsu Hô.* Hani's remarks, also censored material, is in the same publication. A personal letter to my research assistant contains the statements of Mrs. Yukie Kimoto. Kenichi Tada's remarks are in a censored, unpublished article, "Philosophy of Destruction," found in *Shuppan Keisatsu Hô.* The quotes of Miss Yoshida are in a letter to the author from Miss Wells. Material relating to the actions of Kazuko Suzuki comes from an interview in Tokyo. Reference to the British Embassy is in Grew's *Ten Years.* The activity of the factory owner's wife is reported in U. S. Strategic Bombing Survey, *The Effects of Strategic Bombing on Japanese Morale* (1947).

The findings of the legal section, First Demolition Ministry, are in "Damages Sustained in the Air Attack 18 April 1942," a document presented as evidence at the International Military Tribunal, Far East. Information on the operations of Japanese planes and surface units is in "Homeland Defense Naval Operations, December 1941–March 1943," *Japanese Monograph No. 109*, No. 1. The radio station JOAK quote comes from the *Japan Times and Advertiser*, 20 April 1942. For the effect of the raid on Japanese morale, the author also consulted the lengthy letter and memo written by Col. T. J. Betts to Asst. Chief of Staff, G-2, 20 April 1942; and memo from Robert S. Spencer to Col. Bicknell, 22 May 1942. Both of these letters are in the National Archives. The *New York Times* of 19 April 1942 describes the raid's effect on Chungking and Harrison Forman's activities.

The official reports of Watson and Scott, Scott's statements in the *New York Times*, 28 June 1942, and interviews are the basis for the description of Watson's fight with enemy cruisers. Doolittle's quote is from Reynolds' *Doolittle*. The bail-out scene is reconstructed from material in the reports of Doolittle, Potter, Leonard, and Braemer.

ESCAPE

109–116   The sergeant's quote is in "Details of Individual Ad-
132–139   ventures in China," which is included in Cooper's Report. Reference to the area of Japanese-occupied China is from Marshall's history. The experiences of Doolittle and his crew in China, including the quotes, are from their official reports and from Reynolds' *Doolittle*. The actions of Hoover's, Gray's, Holstrom's, and Jones' crews are recounted in their official reports, statements made in interviews with Captain McGhee, interviews, "Details of Individual Adventures in China" in Cooper's Report, and remarks in the *New York Times*, 25 January, 25 April 1943. Data for reconstructing Hallmark's plane crash comes from Nielsen's testimony at the International Military Tribunal, Far East, his statements in the *New York Times*, 26 August 1945, and Watson's *DeShazer*. Cora Houston's account is in the *New York Times*, 25 October 1942.

116–120   The material regarding Lawson and his crew is
139–143   from Thatcher's report, Davenport's remarks to Major

160–162   Pinkney, White's reports and his diary, and *Thirty*
167–172   *Seconds over Tokyo*. The adventures of York's crew
in Russia are described in Emmen's *Guests of the Kremlin*.

120–126   Sections dealing with Joyce's crew in China are
143–147   based on the report of Joyce, statements in the *New York Times*, 25 April 1943, and "For Public Relations Branch. When, As and If War Department Thinks Proper," which is attached to Cooper's Report. Parts detailing the activities of Watson's crew and those of Bower, McElroy, Greening, and Hilger come from the official reports; interviews; statements made to Major Pinkney and Captain McGhee; statements in the *New York Times*, 28 June 1942; 22, 23, 25 April 1943; *Life Magazine*, 3 May 1943; *Time Magazine*, 3 May 1943; and Eierman's article in *Popular Science*.

126–130   The description of the action of Don Smith and his
147–152   men is related in the official reports, White's diary, his article in *Atlantic*, interviews, and "For Public Relations Branch. When, As and If War Department Thinks Proper," which is included in Cooper's Report.

130–131   DeShazer relates his experiences in Watson's *DeShazer;* Barr tells about the capture in his testimony for the International Military Tribunal, Far East; Private Kumano's statement also comes from the testimony before the Tribunal.

152–157   Material relating to the captured airmen comes
passim.   from the testimony of Barr and Nielsen and other evidence presented at the war crimes' trials, DeShazer's statements in Watson's *DeShazer*, remarks in the *Washington Post*, 24 April 1943, and in the *New York Times*, 26, and 30 August 1945, 6 September 1945.

158, 159–   The data regarding Doolittle is from his official re-
160, 165   port, the Cooper Report, Marshall's history, and Reynolds' *Doolittle*. The Japanese massacre in Chinese territory is described by Rev. George Yager, American missionary, in the *New York Times*, 26 May 1943. Additional material was obtained from interviews and

from the *New York Times,* 29 April 1943 and from Marshall's history. The statement regarding the captured airmen bearing the responsibility for all the raid's bombing errors is also in Samuel Eliot Morison's *The Rising Sun in the Pacific, 1931–April 1942* (History of United States Naval Operations in World War II, vol. III, 1955), pp. 395–396.

162, 165   John Birch's actions are described in his official
179–180   statement in Cooper's Report. Doolittle's quote while in Chungking comes from "For Public Relations Branch. When, As, and If War Department Thinks Proper," attached to Cooper's Report. Doolittle's speech in the epilogue is best found in a War Department press release, Bureau of Public Relations. Japanese strategy discussed in the epilogue is based on "Homeland Defense Naval Operations, December 1941–March 1943," *Japanese Monograph No. 109,* Part 1; and the interrogations of Captains Watanabe and Ohmae, IJN, in U. S. Strategic Bombing Survey, *Interrogations of Japanese Officials,* Naval Analysis Division, Vol. I.

INDEX

PRINTED IN U.S.A.

ULISYS

12231932

Ex-Library: Friends of
Lake County Public Library

X

LAKE COUNTY PUBLIC LIBRARY
INDIANA

940.5442   MERR   64   C. 4
MERRILL   J.M.   4.95
TARGET TOKYO

BO	GR		NC
CE	HI	JUL 11 73	RF
CL	HO		SC
DY	IH		SJ
EG	ME		AV
FF	MU		

TO RENEW, PLEASE GIVE ALL INFORMATION SHOWN ABOVE.